Church Fathers, Independent Virgins

JOYCE E. SALISBURY

VERSO

London · New York

First published by Verso 1991
© Joyce E. Salisbury 1991

Verso
UK: 6 Meard Street, London W1V 3HR
USA: 29 West 35th Street, New York, NY 10001-2291

Verso is the imprint of New Left Books

British Library Cataloguing in Publication Data
Salisbury, Joyce E.
   Church fathers, independent virgins.
   1. Sex relations. Attitudes of christian church, history
   I. Title
   261.835

   ISBN 0-86091-293-0

US Library of Congress Cataloging-in-Publication Data
Salisbury, Joyce E.
   Church fathers, independent virgins / Joyce E. Salisbury.
      p.   cm.
   Includes bibliographical references and index.
   ISBN 0-86091-293-0
    1. Virginity—Religious aspects—Christianity—History of
doctrines—Early church, ca. 30–600. 2. Sex—Religious aspects—
—Christianity—History of doctrines—Early church, ca. 30–600.
3. Sex role—Religious aspects—Christianity—History of doctrines—
Early church, ca. 30–600.   4. Women in Christianity—History—Early
church, ca. 30–600. I. Title.
BR195.C45S24   1991
261.8'357'09—dc20

Printed in Great Britain by Bookcraft (Bath) Ltd
Typeset in Times Roman by Leaper & Gard Ltd

Contents

Acknowledgements

In 1984 I was fortunate to participate in a National Endowment for the Humanities Summer Seminar, "Women in Medieval Life and Literature" at Columbia University, led by Professor Joan Ferrante. During this time I began the early work on this book, and its conception was forwarded by conversations and advice from Professor Ferrante and other participants in the seminar, especially Professor Joan Cadden of Kenyon College.

My colleagues throughout the State of Wisconsin also offered support and advice. I particularly thank Professor James Brundage, who generously shared his knowledge of manuscript work and expertise in the history of sexuality. Professor Julie Brickley brought experience gained from years of study and teaching women and religion to a careful reading of the manuscript. Professor Jane Schulenburg's unflagging encouragement helped me continue the task. Finally, Professor Harvey Kaye offered the advice and support necessary to bring the book to press.

The abbot at the Escorial monastery near Madrid generously allowed me to have the precious manuscript microfilmed so I could work on it slowly with the care it required.

For material support, I was the recipient of Les and Corky Blumberg's generous hospitality, when they let me use their beautiful, tranquil farmhouse in New Holstein as a research retreat.

Finally, the dedication is for my mother, who by example taught me what I know about integrity, responsibility, and perseverance.

To Grace

Introduction

In the late fourth century, Augustine wrote a letter to a chaste matron, Ecdicia. Some years earlier, Ecdicia had persuaded her reluctant husband to join her in a vow of chastity to live a "spiritual marriage" instead of a carnal one. Ecdicia's husband fell from his vow and took a mistress; the aggrieved wife wrote to Augustine seeking advice, and no doubt sympathy. Augustine's response in the surviving letter was surely not what Ecdicia had expected, for he reprimanded the woman, saying: "This great evil [the adultery] arose from your not treating him in his state of mind with the moderation you should have shown. ..."[1] Ecdicia had apparently assumed that her vow of chastity released her from other wifely responsibilities, notably that of obedience to her husband. Without consulting him, Ecdicia gave a good part of her property to two wandering monks, causing him to fly into a rage and curse her for subverting his authority and depriving their son of some of his patrimony. That was not the full extent of Ecdicia's disobedience. In her piety (or willfulness, depending on one's point of view) she chose to put aside a fitting "matronly costume" and wear widow's clothing while her husband was still living.

Augustine showed a good deal of sympathy for the husband, who had taken the vow of chastity reluctantly in the first place and had been driven to anger by his wife's subsequent behavior. The Bishop wrote: "Finally, it came about that, when scorned, he [the husband] broke the bond of continence which he had taken upon himself when he was loved, and in his anger at you he did not spare himself."[2] Augustine advised Ecdicia to apologize to her husband, to promise to obey him and submit to his will in all things except the carnal debt which they had both renounced. Augustine felt that in this way the husband could be won back to a chaste marriage and the wife, by being humble and obedient, could establish a truly virtuous life consistent with his view of her vow of chastity.

1

This account represents more than a fourth-century example of domestic disharmony. It shows a serious struggle that took place from the late second century at least through the fourth century regarding the role of celibate women in society. Ecdicia seems to have believed that by renouncing the marriage debt and taking control over her own body, she could also control other aspects of her life. Her husband and Augustine did not agree with her. They believed that her renunciation of sexuality did not mean that she was freed from other feminine obligations, primarily that of subservience.

In this book, I shall explore these differing views of chastity. However, too often works studying virginity and chastity have treated those topics as if they were somehow separate from sexuality. In fact, perceptions of virginity and how the chaste were to live were derived in large part from views on sexuality and gender roles. Therefore, I shall examine early Christian views of sexuality which shaped men's and women's approaches to chastity. In his important book on law and sex in the Middle Ages, James Brundage identified three patterns of belief about sexual morality that have persisted since the patristic period: sex as reproduction, sex as pollution, and, less often, sex as a source of marital intimacy.[3] However, there was also a fourth way of looking at sex, and this was expressed in the lives of the women I shall describe here. For them, and for others, sex was responsibility, binding them to worldly cares and social roles. Ecdicia seems to have adhered to the fourth pattern of belief, seeing sex as bondage and chastity as release from that bondage. Augustine articulated the culmination of a patristic tradition that combined elements of the first three patterns of sexual belief and confronted celibate men and women who claimed independence from social expectations based upon the spirituality of their lives.

Ecdicia's position came from an ascetic tradition that spread west from the Holy Land, the Syrian deserts and Egypt.[4] The ascetic tradition was one in which individuals removed themselves from society by physical renunciations and, by so doing, acquired spiritual power.[5] Once they gained such power, most ascetic holy people believed they had established their right to seek God in their own fashion. They placed themselves outside the hierarchic structure of the Church, and frequently believed themselves exempt from the requirements of obedience to authority. These individuals, both men and women, were highly respected by the faithful because of their spiritual power, which at times was exerted in the form of miracles to benefit the community. By the second century, the ascetic tradition becomes visible in surviving written works. One of the central hallmarks of this tradition was the strong advocacy of virginity or chastity as the primary renunciation that separated potential holy people from society. In the second century, this stress on virginity appeared in various places. First of all, the Gnostic school in Alexandria provided a clearly argued stand for the importance of virginity. John Bugge, in his excellent analysis of the tradition of virginity, stressed the importance of the Gnostic tradition, seeing in it the "soul of monasticism" which equated "virginity with the ontological state of prelapsarian human nature."[6] Gnostics may have presented the clearest argument within the theological stress on virginity, but they were not the only ones advocating chastity.

The earliest Apocryphal Acts of the Apostles, those of John, Paul, and probably Peter, were composed in the second century. These were followed in the third century by the Acts of Andrew and Thomas. All these Apocryphal Acts strongly advocated chastity as the preferred way of life. For example, in the Acts of Thomas, a follower summarized Thomas's thought as follows: "Thou teachest, saying that men cannot live well except they live chastely. ..."[7] These Acts were so adamant about rejecting the flesh that the Manichaeans incorporated them into their sacred texts. The Acts themselves may have suited the Manichaean anti-carnal position, but they originally derived from an ascetic theology that began to be articulated as early as the composition of the orthodox Gospels and Acts. This tradition continued to have adherents, so that Acts of apostles based on the early five Apocryphal Acts continued to be composed in monasteries in the fifth century and even later, particularly in Egypt.[8] The ascetic tradition that was being articulated in these early Christian centuries appealed to both men and women. For men, asceticism usually required more than just sexual renunciation, although that was often the initial prerequisite. Would-be holy men acquired power by transcending physical needs and demonstrating heroic feats of ascetic renunciation, including fasts and other deprivations. The tradition of ascetic men may be followed from the third century in the East from Antony of Egypt, the literary prototype, through the stylites and other desert fathers, whose sayings had been recorded, copied, and widely circulated even in the West.

Because of gender preconceptions, the ascetic tradition for men and women was not the same. For example, it was perfectly possible for male ascetics to advocate independence from ecclesiastical authority for themselves based on the power they achieved through ascetic renunciation, while at the same time denying women ascetics the same right. Nevertheless, women were claiming the right for such independence for themselves. The problem was compounded by the fact that women claiming freedom from ecclesiastical authority seem to have believed that such independence also exempted them from expected women's social roles. This was the problem Augustine had with Ecdicia; he believed her chastity did not release her from feminine obedience to her husband. The fundamental difference between male and female ascetics, then, was that men did not renounce their social positions of power; women did want to renounce their positions of impotence.

In this work, I shall focus on the ascetic tradition as it applied to women. It is likely that the Apocryphal Acts of the Apostles represented the earliest surviving written expression of the female ascetic position. Stevan Davies makes a well-argued case that the Apocryphal Acts were composed by women living ascetic, or at least celibate lives.[9] In fact, he argues that "We find in the Acts a positive and fairly realistic view of female Christians, which could serve to bolster, not to undermine, the self-image of women in the Church."[10] This is precisely the position that ascetic women were shaping for themselves during the unstructured early centuries of Christianity, but they were not simply improving their self-image. They were embracing an asceticism that allowed them to create lives for themselves that were free from socially expected patterns of behavior.

During the early centuries of Christianity, women took various paths to an independent spiritual life. The Apocryphal Acts portrayed one kind of woman's position, that of praising celibacy as the *sine qua non* of a Christian life. For these women, the renunciation of their sexuality and the preservation of their virginity or even chastity was enough to confer some measure of power,[11] power over their own bodies and, by extension, over their own lives. This seems to have been true in Ecdicia's case, at least in her perception. Jo Ann McNamara has examined the ascetic tradition as it was practiced by women in the first two centuries of Christianity and concluded that "The unstructured new religion that spread through the Empire offered, among its other attractions, a strong individualistic message which some women used to ... create a positive new identity grounded in celibacy, and transcending the gender system."[12]

Other women chose to perform feats of asceticism and follow a path of sanctity similar to those of their ascetic brothers. In the ninth century, for example, one hundred women lived as stylites in a Syrian monastery,[13] which was a renunciation as extreme as any. But even by patterning themselves after male ascetics these women were breaking new ground; women were not supposed to be able to perform such "masculine" feats. However, as Margot King has demonstrated, the Egyptian desert seems to have been virtually populated with female ascetics,[14] and the female anchoretic tradition continued throughout the Middle Ages. The persistent practice of female asceticism was well established by the second century, when enough women had chosen to remain celibate for orders of virgins and widows to be accepted, albeit at times reluctantly, by established Church authorities.

Church Fathers were placed in a curious dilemma when they explored the ideal of virginity and considered the position of women living a chaste life. On the one hand, they strongly supported the ideal of virginity. There was a sufficiently strong bias against the flesh in the Scriptures, particularly in the writings of Paul, to provide a theoretical basis for advocating celibacy. However, the advocacy of virginity and ascetic renunciation in general was leading to the presence of holy women assuming an independence that was unacceptable to the Fathers.

Church Fathers objected to women's independence for two general reasons. First, an obvious threat to homogeneity was posed by individuals not directly under ecclesiastic control,[15] and this applied to both male and female ascetics. Independent women, however, posed another, more subtle threat to churchmen (and laymen, for that matter). Independent women practicing celibacy disturbed the Fathers' understanding of gender roles and of sexuality itself, which added an additional imperative to patristic regulation of women. In the classical age, which shaped patristic views, male sexuality and power were closely associated,[16] and female sexuality was associated with passivity. If a woman's sexuality defined her gender as subservient, how was that reconciled with her asceticism, which accrued power for her? The question was a serious one, for the power relationship between men and women was seen as fundamental to an appropriate ordering of the world.

For example, Isidore of Seville, the last of the Latin Fathers, said that women were softer and weaker than men, but if by chance a woman should be stronger than a particular man and successfully resist him, he would be driven by his lust to seek a partner of his own sex.[17] Thus a reversal of power would lead to gender reversal and drive a man to become the passive partner in a homosexual encounter, and such passivity was defined as effeminate. This disaster on the individual level could be reproduced on a larger societal level if the reversal were large-scale.

An example drawn from the late reformers' reflections on the subject vividly expresses the fears early churchmen shared with them. The reformers determined that Noah's Flood was caused by people having intercourse in the woman-superior position.[18] Reversals of the "natural" order of sexual power could even have cosmic repercussions, calling forth a flood. So the task of the Fathers was to reconcile their views on sexuality and power with the reality of chastity and power. In the first half of this book, I shall analyze the ways in which this reconciliation was achieved, for the Latin Fathers did work out a theoretical position that would let them preserve the ideal of virginity and yet keep celibate women subservient.

The theory which argued for control of holy women that Church

Fathers were advocating in the third and fourth centuries slowly began to be put into practice by legislation from the fourth through the sixth centuries. For example, as early as the beginning of the fourth century churchmen at the Council of Elvira in Spain began to legislate for widows and virgins, requiring them to take public vows and wear prescribed, identifiable clothing;[19] and to begin to bring women, who had previously followed their consciences in these matters, under the rule of law. In Spain, this movement toward control culminated in a seventh-century monastic reform movement which, at least theoretically, placed all ascetics under the direct control of their respective bishops,[20] thus finally ideally bringing independent holy people within the sphere of hierarchical authority. The legislation in Spain had its parallel all over Western Europe. Monastic legislation testifies to what was essentially a victory of the patristic position over the independent ascetic one. In this spirit, Augustine wrote reprimanding Ecdicia for her independent actions.

However, when dealing with the history of ideas, one cannot say that the institutionalizing of one set of ideas necessarily led to the obliteration of another. The Fathers may have had the power of Church and state behind their decrees, but the concept of an independent ascetic ideal for women survived. One measure of the survival of the ideal was that many women continued to – or at least attempted to – live reasonably independent lives purchased by their renunciation of sexuality. The example of Ecdicia hints at one such woman, but there were many others throughout the Middle Ages.[21]

In writing of the early Church, Jo Ann McNamara noted that "The women who were the objects of so much of their [Church Fathers'] teaching remain silent, but their deeds still speak to us."[22] The deeds of many of these women were preserved in saints' lives. Some of these women's saints' lives followed in the tradition of the Apocryphal Acts of the Apostles, which also advocated the female ascetic tradition. Further testimony to the survival of the ascetic ideal even among those who were unable to live out such an ideal is that these saints' lives were treasured, copied and recopied. One example of the value which these narratives were accorded can be seen in a seventh-century Syrian manuscript discovered and translated in the late nineteenth century by Agnes Smith Lewis. This manuscript contained the Lives of four holy women (Eugenia, Mary, Onesima and Euphrosyne) whose deeds expressed the ascetic ideal of power and independence earned by sexual renunciation. The scribe who had wanted to record these Lives in the seventh century did not have enough vellum to do so, so he or she created a palimpsest, scraping a Gospel to erase it and writing the Lives over it.[23] The sacrifice of a Gospel to preserve ascetic women's lives surely bears witness to the desire to preserve an ascetic ideal. The ideal was not preserved only in the copying; these Lives were apparently much read. As Lewis observed of the manuscript: "The thumb-marks which discolour the margins of the manuscript, always at a similar part of each page, bear a silent testimony to their popularity. ..."[24] It is the ascetic women's tradition expressed in saints' lives such as these that I shall analyze and juxtapose with the patristic tradition.

Just as the patristic writings circulated widely, so did women's saints' lives. In order to choose from the wide array of lives available, I have decided to focus my study on those found in one codex. These Lives are bound in a tenth-century manuscript kept in the Escorial monastic library outside Madrid.[25] This collection contains the Lives of seven women who exemplify the Eastern ascetic tradition, in which women took independence and sovereignty for granted as consequences of their vows of chastity. Two of the Lives, those of Helia and Egeria, were probably written in Spain. The others, those of Mary of Egypt, Melania the Younger, Pelagia, Castissima, and Constantina, came from the East. Early in the tenth century, someone in northern Spain gathered the Lives from various manuscripts, and copied them together. This collection remained together and was recopied for centuries. It is reasonable to believe that these Lives were put together and kept together because they had certain commonalities – for example, they were all women, and none was a martyr (which is somewhat surprising, since there were a number of popular narratives of martyrs' Passions circulating in Spain at the time, and most of the collections of saints' lives contained them). An additional commonality is that the Lives collected in this manuscript are representative of the female ascetic tradition, and I shall use them to analyze a view of womanhood, chastity, and sexuality different from that of the Church Fathers.

It is important to recognize that this view of independent, ascetic women did not appeal only to women; this is not only a "women's view" (although there is such a view implicit within the Lives). The manuscripts that preserve these Lives were sometimes copied by women (the nun Leodegúndia copied one of the Lives in the ninth century[26]) and sometimes by men (the monk John copied the whole corpus in the tenth century[27]). They appeal to both because they reflect an ascetic view that was popular for both some men and some women, so presumably when men were admiring the Lives they saw in them ascetic lessons for themselves. That does not change the fact that they demonstrated models for women that were strikingly different from patristic models for female behavior. Fortunately for us, the elements that appealed to ascetics of both genders probably helped to preserve this view for us. The Spanish ascetic tradition for men and women that was saved in this manuscript was not unique in Europe. It was strongly influenced by thought from the East, and many of the saints' lives that make up this manuscript were the same ones that were eventually popular all over Western Europe.

In sum, our Christian heritage includes several views of sexuality and continence as applied to women. There were two general patristic positions: that of the early Fathers, and that of Augustine. The Augustinian model became predominant, influencing not only the Christian Church but the Christian society which forms one of the underpinnings of our Western culture. The tremendous influence of patristic works has, to a large degree, made us forget that Augustine's model was not the only perspective that persisted throughout the Middle Ages. The older ascetic tradition for women that dignified womanhood and offered a larger degree of independence for celibate women also endured, and remains part of our heritage.

This book explores all three views of virginity and the views of sex that underlay them. The first part looks at the Fathers, describing their views of sexuality and their rules for virgins that derived from their vision. The second part begins by exploring the ways the women in the Lives expressed their independence in violation of patristic prescriptions. Finally, the last chapter describes the theoretical base that establishes the unifying principles behind all the Lives. This is the alternative view of sexuality and womanhood that stands beside that of the Fathers. In this way I hope to help recapture the diversity that formed our Christian culture – a diversity that produced not only an Augustine, but an Ecdicia and her spiritual sisters.

PART I

The Fathers

1

The Early Fathers on Sexuality: The Carnal World

The ideas that have prevailed in the Christian Church in the West were in large part shaped by a handful of men, theological giants who slowly built Christian thought into a complex, highly structured body of ideas that dominated the medieval world. These men commented on many aspects of Christian life and thought, but they did not all agree on Christian doctrine or practice.

For example, Tertullian, in the late second century in North Africa, urged the faithful to break with the pagan past and trust the Spirit over authority. In the mid-third century, Tertullian's spiritual heir in North Africa, Cyprian, built upon his master but modified Tertullian's thought to incorporate a belief in obedience to the hierarchic authority of a bishop. By the late fourth century, Christian thinkers were not so certain that the world was going to end immediately. Men like Ambrose and Jerome turned their attention to the Church on earth, and among their many contributions they brought asceticism to the West. These two influential thinkers worked independently, although virtually contemporaneously, to incorporate the ideas of Eastern asceticism and Christian chastity into Western practice. Ambrose accented Christian Platonism, while Jerome staunchly rejected any study of classical learning for Christians. Yet both arrived at similar values for Christian virgins, and both were influential in articulating those values for later generations. While Tertullian, Cyprian, Ambrose and Jerome differed in many aspects of their thought, they were all products of the late Roman view of sexuality and they all struggled to reject Roman acceptance of carnality to establish a new Christian vision of sex. As diverse as their ideas were on many other issues, they shared the same view of sexuality.

During the centuries after the birth of Christ, when Christianity spread through the Roman Empire, Christians had to reassess their position in the world. To what degree did their conversion make them different from pagan Romans? In some things it was easy to reject Roman values. Christians could avoid violent games and luxurious conspicuous consumption. Other things, however, required more thought. A Christian might reject the licentious sexuality that marked Rome, but sexuality itself was too central to human beings to be dismissed as easily as a gladiator match. As James Brundage observed in his important work on law and sex in medieval Europe, Christian intellectuals had to "... account for the place of sex in the scheme of creation and to define the role that sexual relations ought to play in the Christian life."[1] S. Laeuchli, in his study *Power and Sexuality*, argued that there was a crisis of identity in ancient times that led to a crisis in understanding the human position in the world.[2] It was within this identity crisis of Christians in a Roman world that Christian thinkers wrestled with questions of sexuality: was sexuality itself a good or an evil? What was the nature of Christian sexuality? What place did sexual intercourse have in a Christian marriage? What was the nature of Christian celibacy? What was the role of celibates in a Christian society? These and related questions seemed central to understanding the human condition, and called forth reflection by some of the greatest Christian thinkers of the ancient world.

Some of the most important writers in the West on such matters were Tertullian, Cyprian, Ambrose, Jerome and Augustine. They referred to each other's works, built upon each other's thought, sometimes disagreed, but together created a body of thought that established a Christian understanding of many of the issues that shaped Christian society, among them human sexuality and its mirror image, holy celibacy.

The first four Church Fathers (Tertullian, Cyprian, Ambrose and Jerome) shared a fundamental view of sexuality, and this view was basically dualistic. That is to say, these Fathers saw a clear division between that which was carnal (sexual) and that which was not (spiritual). It is important to recognize that I am not using the word "dualistic" to suggest that these early Fathers adhered to the Gnostic dualism that would trouble orthodox Christianity off and on for centuries. That heretical dualism located a dichotomy of good and evil in a heaven inhabited by a good and an evil God. The early Fathers recognized only spirituality and goodness in the heavens. Their dualist perspective applied only to earth, and only to earth after the Fall.

The dualistic dichotomy between flesh and spirit is complicated by the fact that the most spiritual of people have bodies – as Jerome used Paul's metaphor, "we have our treasure in earthen vessels."[3] The Fathers did not necessarily equate flesh with the visible body. Spirit and flesh were opposite abstract principles that could be understood by their expression in concrete actions – for example prayer, or sexual intercourse. In a sense, the terms flesh and spirit represented potential states that the body could actualize. The body itself was neutral and could be drawn to either the flesh or the spirit, depending on which urges the individual followed. Cyprian wrote to virgins whose sexual renunciation had placed them in the realm of spiritual things, and his pronouncements repeatedly reminded them that their bodies had become spiritual. He said that by "renouncing the concupiscence of the flesh, [they] have dedicated themselves to God in body as well as in spirit. ..."[4] After a woman's sexual renunciation, Cyprian could refer to the "sanctity of her body,"[5] and in a similar spirit, Ambrose and Jerome could refer to a virgin's body as the "temple of God."[6] Just as the incarnation had made Christ's body and blood worthy of veneration, so a spiritual life could convert the individual's body into a vehicle of sanctity. For the Fathers, then, a spiritual life could bring about a resurrection of the body while on earth, in imitation of the bodily resurrection to come.

It is this capacity of the body to partake in the spiritual that makes comprehensible the very real veneration of the body that was expressed in cults of saints' relics that were becoming so popular[7] at the same time as the Church Fathers were writing so prolifically and powerfully about the irreconcilable dichotomy between flesh and spirit. Saints' relics were the tangible remnants of a spiritual life that had been so thoroughly acted upon that spirituality in the form of power to perform miracles remained in the sanctified body. The body, then, was exempt from the ontological dualism of flesh versus spirit. The body could become a temple of God – or, in Jerome's words, it could become a brothel in which the "members of Christ" had been "prostituted."[8]

To understand the nature of the flesh as the Fathers did, we must begin with the Fall of humanity from the Garden of Eden. The early Fathers saw the Fall as somehow connected to sexuality. The logic was inexorable for Jerome, for "before the Fall, Adam and Eve were virgins in Paradise, but after they had sinned, and were cast out of Paradise, they were immediately married."[9] Marriage conjured up negative images; the Fathers warned of the trials of marriage for women: caring for children, ordering the house and pleasing a husband.[10] Most of all, since these thinkers saw Adam and Eve's original sin as sexual, marriage brought forth its own sexual consequences, the fact that one no longer had control over one's own body. Marriage not only bound men and women together but bound them together sexually, a carnal bond which tied both bodies to the world of the flesh. Each partner was in debt to the other and had to pay literally in flesh to satisfy the other's carnal desires.[11] And, as Jerome noted with his usual lack of delicacy, "There is no greater calamity connected with captivity [of marriage] than to be the victim of another's lust."[12] Ascetic women shared this fear of marital bondage, but the Fathers grounded their rejection in a more profound repudiation of the flesh. For early Fathers, marriage did not change the reality that in a world split between good and evil, spirit and flesh, sex was evil. Consider Tertullian's statement: "It is laws which seem to make the difference between marriage and fornication; through diversity of illicitness, not through the nature of the thing itself."[13] Even though he was married, Tertullian believed sexuality was "illicit" regardless of the legal status of marriage. He did not hold a high opinion of the carnal bond between man and wife.

Without the Fall, this carnal bond would not have existed. People could have remained in the spiritual state in which they had been created. However, the spiritual state that the Fathers presented in such a contrast to the carnal state of marriage was accessible even to fallen humanity. First of all, it was knowable through people's understanding of the angelic life in heaven. All the Fathers explained repeatedly that angels were asexual, with no trace of earthly flesh to mar their spiritual existences.[14] Furthermore, the Fathers taught that after the resurrection there would be no more marriage,[15] with its carnal obligations. As Jerome explained the afterlife, "we shall either be of no sex as are the angels, or at all events ... though we rise from the dead in our own sex, we shall not perform the functions of sex."[16] If the spiritual life had once been possible for men and women in their prelapsarian state, and if it would be again their lot after the resurrection, then it made sense to strive for that state while in the world, even in the fallen world. As Tertullian urged, "For, if we must glory in something, let it be the spirit rather than the flesh that we wish to please. ..."[17]

Since according to the Fathers the main consequence of the Fall had been to introduce a preoccupation with sex, the way to recapture the angelic life was to strive for an asexual existence – ideally virginity, or at least chastity. All the Fathers repeatedly stressed that virginity reproduced the angelic life here on earth, and they wrote of it in such encomiastic terms that no one would think the virgin life was anything less than a pure angelic existence. Cyprian said: "While you remain chaste and virgins you are equal to the angels of God ...,"[18] and Ambrose made the dichotomy even clearer: "For chastity has made even angels. He who has preserved it is an angel; he who has lost it a devil."[19] Thus for the Fathers there were two realms available to people on earth after the Fall, the spiritual and the carnal. These two realms had nothing in common, and this sharp distinction between the two reveals the Fathers' dualistic perception of the world and of the sexuality introduced into the world at the Fall.

The carnal and the spiritual realms were opposites, and as such were mutually exclusive. The completeness of the incompatibility of the two states was such that activities which pertained to one realm precluded participation in activities properly belonging to the other. For example, drawing from the writings of Paul, the Fathers felt that one could not pray unless one had abstained from sexual intercourse.[20] Since intercourse was carnal, it precluded participation in prayer, which was spiritual. The two states were profoundly opposite, and opposites could not coexist in the same moment. It is this dualistic view of the nature of sexuality that underlay the Church's developing advocacy of clerical celibacy.

The dualistic nature of the human condition caused the individual to be torn between the spiritual and the carnal. Ambrose described a perpetual war within people between the spirit and the flesh,[21] which meant that each person had to choose at any moment in which realm he or she would participate. Of course, the Fathers advocated the victory of the spiritual (which they frequently identified as being located in the mind) over the carnal (usually located in the body). Tertullian could have spoken for all of them when he cried: "Renounce we things carnal, that we may at length bear fruits spiritual."[22] The mutual exclusivity of the two realms provided the key for the victory over the flesh. By choosing to participate in spiritual things to the fullest degree possible, the individual would have no room for the carnal. As Jerome explained to Eustochium, who was struggling to preserve her virginity and live a spiritual life: "The love of the flesh is overcome by the love of the spirit. Desire is quenched by desire. What is taken from the one increases the other."[23]

This statement might recall a Freudian model of sublimated sexuality, but to impose such a model on the early Fathers would be to misunderstand the degree to which they saw the spiritual as distinct from the carnal. Sublimation provides a mechanism by which people can control sexual acts, but sublimation remains sexuality, albeit sexuality turned to another purpose. The Fathers believed it possible, albeit very difficult, to escape sexuality itself and participate in a realm uncorrupted by sexuality, untouched by the carnal.

Even though, as we have seen, the body had the capacity to be spiritual while still in this life, it was very difficult. Jerome warned that "... as long as we dwell in the tabernacle of this body, ... we are enveloped with this fragile flesh. ..."[24] Indeed, the flesh called to the body and lured it to the carnal. The core of this carnal realm was sexuality, and the Fathers understood sexuality in strongly physical terms,[25] which further highlighted the difference between the flesh and the spirit. The carnal, sexual realm lured people through a strong physical appeal to the senses. Ambrose warned of the lure of the senses in his explanation of the biblical passage in which God was described as breathing into man's face. Ambrose explained that the face "... is the seat and abode and enticement of lust – in the eyes, the ears, the nostrils, the mouth – [God breathed there] in order to fortify our senses against such lust."[26] The senses, then, would lead people into sexuality, which would bind them to the physical, carnal realm at the expense of the spiritual.

The sensual metaphors with which the Fathers warned of the dangers of lust reveal a good deal about their perceptions of the strong physical nature of the carnal world that lured people to the flesh. Jerome warned strongly against the sense of touch. Any man who wanted to strive for spiritual things had better avoid even the slightest contact with a woman, however innocent or accidental the touch might be. Jerome saw the danger of touch to be immediate: "As then he who touches fire is instantly burned, so by the mere touch the peculiar nature of man and woman is perceived, and the difference of sex is understood."[27] By "understood" Jerome did not mean understanding with the mind, but a physical "understanding" which called the body to one's attention, thus drawing one away from the spiritual world to the carnal.

This danger of touch was also rather poignantly addressed in the Pseudo-Clementine Epistles on virginity. These letters were addressed to men who wanted to remain virgin and avoid the pitfalls of associating with women as they traveled about living as wandering ascetics. The author of the letters suggested that when men and women virgins were in a position of worshipping together in church, and it came to the point in the service when they were to greet one other by shaking hands, each of them should quickly wrap his or her hands in robes so they could give the salutation in safety.[28] In this way they could avoid the igniting touch that Jerome saw as automatically awakening the flesh. The avoidance of anything pleasantly tactile, then, would help keep the body from being lured by the sense of touch into the realm of the flesh.

Jerome also warned strongly against being lured by the sense of taste into a sensuality that he associated generally with the gastrointestinal tract. He made a close association between a full stomach and lust. He warned: "First the belly is crammed; then the other members are roused."[29] Elsewhere he elaborated: "Everything provocative or indigestible is to be refused. ... There is nothing which so much heats the body and inflames the passions as undigested food and breathing broken with hiccoughs."[30] Hiccoughs could stir the passions because they called attention to the belly, to the physical, which was by definition sexual.

It was not only food that would lure the body into fleshly concerns, but apparently for Jerome oral sensations could do the same thing. This principle and the relationship between physicality and sexuality can perhaps explain one of Jerome's stranger prohibitions. He warned:

... do not, out of affectation, follow the sickly taste of married ladies who now pressing their teeth together, now keeping their lips wide apart, speak with a lisp, and purposely clip their words. ... Accordingly they find pleasure in what I call adultery of the tongue.[31]

Apparently, this particular speech affectation made one more aware of the movement of the tongue in the mouth, which caused the tongue to participate strongly in the physical realm, thus betraying the whole body sexually, and for Jerome that betrayal amounted to committing adultery.

Tertullian seemed particularly to fear the sense of sight. He warned against visual stimulation as a pathway to lust. Tertullian's writings on the veiling of virgins argued that lust came from visual stimulation, so that for a woman to remain truly virgin she needed to remain veiled so that she would not incite anyone to lust for her because of a glance. He said: "... rear a rampart for your sex, which must neither allow your own eyes egress nor ingress to other people's."[32] The Fathers seemed to think that vision posed a particular threat to men, for the sight of a woman would not only "... foster the desire of concupiscence, [and] enkindle the fire of hope ...,"[33] but would provide fuel for a fantasy that would stir sexual desire. Jerome warned a would-be male ascetic to avoid seeing women other than his mother when he visited her home, for "their faces may dwell in your thoughts and so 'a secret wound may fester in your breast'."[34]

Women were described more often as the objects of this visual stimulation rather than being stimulated by viewing young men, but this fact did not exempt them from participating in the sensual visual experience. Tertullian explained that when a man enjoyed looking at a woman and when a woman enjoyed being looked at they were participating in the same lust.[35] They shared equally in the visual carnal experience, even though only one of them need have looked at the other. Of course, Tertullian's solution for this shared lust fell more harshly on women, for he said women should remain veiled. In that way they would avoid the sensual pleasure of being looked at and men would avoid the sensual pleasure of looking. Thus both would more easily stay in the spiritual activities of this world.

Not only could the senses lure one into lust, but if one participated in the carnal there would be physical, sensual consequences. To demonstrate this, Ambrose referred most to the sense of smell. In fact, smell seemed to define the carnal for Ambrose, for all his tracts on virginity contain a seemingly disproportionate number of references to the sense of smell. For example, he referred to the "smell of faith,"[36] and urged the faithful to "breathe the fragrance of the Lord's resurrection."[37] The references multiply, but the significant thing here is that while the spiritual and the physical realms were both accessible in this world, they were so sufficiently different that women indulging in spirituality or physicality bore the physical consequences of a different smell. That is, the body, which became either spiritual or carnal, reflected its state by its smell. Virgins, by choosing the spiritual life over the carnal, could count as one of the concrete benefits the odor of spirituality, which, according to Ambrose, seems to have been somewhat herbal. Ambrose advised virgins to

> ... present your hands to your nostrils and explore with unwearied and ever-watchful alacrity of mind the perfume of your deeds. The smell of your right hand will be musty to you, and your limbs will be redolent with the odour of the resurrection [elsewhere identified as the odour of the Cedars of Lebanon[38]]; your fingers will exude myrrh. ...[39]

Furthermore, he said that Christ "... prefers the fragrance of ... [her] garments, ... to all other perfumes. ..."[40] While Ambrose was speaking here to virgins, he was discussing sexuality at the same time. For him, the physical act of sex which drew people to the carnal had physical consequences, a change in odor. Those who existed in the realm of the flesh bore the "odor of death," while those existing in the spiritual realm bore the "odor of life."[41]

The only sense that does not pervade patristic warnings about sexuality is hearing. It does not seem to have posed as much of a threat as the other senses, nor does it seem as firmly connected to the sensual realm of the carnal. It may be that hearing was more associated with education and spiritual enlightenment that would lead people away from the delights of the flesh and toward the delights of the spirit. This aural educational emphasis is demonstrated by Ambrose, who urged virgins to "keep their ears open"[42] so that they might be led to a virtuous life at the same time as he was insisting that the virginal life required that every other sense remain "closed."

The degree to which the Church Fathers explained the carnal, sexual world in terms of physical sensuality reveals much about their understanding of sexuality and its place in the world. Sex was the center of the "flesh," and all things physical led to sexuality. In fact, all sensual experiences (with the possible exception of auditory ones) were sexual, and this perspective formed the backdrop to patristic understanding of the nature of sexuality. However, in order to identify the enemy of spirituality in their basically dualistic framework, the Fathers also discussed secondary characteristics of sexuality.

For the Fathers, one of the important things to remember about sexuality was that it was natural for fallen humanity to feel lust. "Desire that is implanted in men by God to lead them to procreate children, is internal," wrote Jerome, adding that it was very difficult to "... overcome that which is innate in you. ..."[43] For someone to live a chaste and spiritual life, he or she must "act against nature."[44]

As they spoke of the natural impulse toward sex and the sensual attraction of intercourse, the Fathers acknowledged that another characteristic of sex was that it was pleasurable. Jerome warned: "... lust tickles the sense and the soft fire of sensual pleasure sheds over us its pleasing glow. ..."[45] Ambrose, too, acknowledged that "... carnal intercourse with women is a pleasure and even physicians say it is healthful."[46] The very pleasure of intercourse posed a double danger. First it seduced the body into the carnal realm, but it also worked to prevent people from renouncing the carnal once the sensual pleasures had been experienced. In other words, the Fathers saw sex as habit-forming. Ambrose referred to a "... habit of incontinence ..."[47] and all the Fathers agreed that once one had experienced carnal pleasures, it was hard to stop. The subject comes up most often when they discuss widows, who might have a harder time remaining chaste than virgins, who "... know nothing of the promptings of the flesh. ..."[48] This principle was also expressed vividly by Jerome, who wrote of his experiences when he had gone into the desert and fasted to conquer his own cravings for the flesh in order to choose spirituality. Yet his time in the desert was haunted by recollections of his previous experiences:

> [In the desert] ... where I had no companions but scorpions and wild beasts, I often found myself amid bevies of girls. My face was pale and my frame chilled with fasting; yet my mind was burning with desire, and the fire of lust kept bubbling up before me when my flesh was as good as dead.[49]

Jerome's experience perhaps explains his fear of the lure and power of experienced sexuality. He spoke for all the Fathers when he warned that "Passion ... is never satisfied, and once quenched it is soon kindled anew. Its growth or decay is a matter of habit. ..."[50]

These characteristics of sexuality – that it is natural, pleasurable and almost irresistible – were articulated to make people aware of the difficulties in struggling against the carnal. They did not provide a way to battle against the lure of the flesh. The Fathers did, however, identify a sexual characteristic that would help people in their struggle for the spiritual. A principal characteristic of sex was that it was hot; thus one could avoid anything hot to help cool sexual ardor. To be heated or burned was one of the metaphors for sex most often used by the early Fathers. Jerome explicitly said: "Our foe uses the heat of youthful passion to tempt young men and maidens ...,"[51] and elsewhere:

'. . . natural heat inevitably kindles in a man sensual passion. . . ."[52] As is frequently the case in medieval thought, the metaphor could also become concrete. If sex were hot, then anything else that was hot led to sexuality. For example, hot baths would kindle young blood[53] and lead youth to sin.

Even more dangerous for rousing heated desire were food and wine, which shared with sex the property of heat. "Neither the fiery Etna nor the country of Vulcan nor Vesuvius, nor Olympus, burns with such violent heat as the youthful marrow of those who are flushed with wine and filled with food."[54] Food was doubly dangerous because not only did it generate heat and thus associate the body with heated sexuality, but it was sensually gratifying, which in turn drew the body into the realm of the senses, which by definition was sexual. For Jerome and the early Fathers a glutton could not be chaste even if he or she abstained from intercourse, because by indulging in the heat and sensuality of an abundance of food one was in fact separated from the spiritual and thus placed in the carnal world.

However, food was not the only source of heat. The Fathers also saw other passions as having the property of heat, so these passions too were united with the primal sin of sexuality. Ambrose cautioned: "A dangerous fire is lust; a dangerous fire is every flame of unjust desire; a dangerous fire is all the heat of greed."[55] Similarly, Jerome urged avoiding "burning with covetousness."[56] To avoid the sins of the flesh, then, one had to avoid everything that was hot – whether actually hot, like a bath or a meal, or metaphorically hot, like a temper.

Given that sexuality had the property of heat, even those who were unable to resist the lure of the flesh in their youth might hope to reach a greater degree of spirituality in their old age, because the Fathers believed, with Galen, that the bodies of the young were hotter than those of the elderly.[57] Therefore, it was in youth that all the passions, including lust, burned most fiercely. With age the body cooled, as did the passions. Accordingly, the Fathers felt that it would be easier for a menopausal woman to remain a widow than for a younger woman. Ambrose described such a woman in language that contrasts with the heat metaphor that permeates his descriptions of sexuality: ". . . worn out in body, cold in age, of ripe years, [who] can neither grow warm with pleasures, nor hope for offspring."[58] Thus for the Fathers another related characteristic of sexuality was that it waned with age, cooling as the body cooled, and presumably in this way the elderly would move closer to the spiritual realm as they neared death.

As the Fathers wrote their tracts on virginity and chastity they felt that they were writing from the spiritual realm, and observing sexuality from the outside. Writing from this perspective, they noted one final characteristic of sexuality. Viewed from the spiritual realm, sex is generally disgusting and degrading. This constrasts sharply with the pleasures of sex that the Fathers described, but the contrast simply parallels the constrast between the spiritual and the carnal. From the standpoint of the spiritual, Jerome could say: "The truth is that, in view of the purity of the body of Christ, all sexual intercourse is unclean."[59] The goal for which the Fathers urged people to strive was to have such disregard for all things carnal that the most pleasurable act was considered "foul" and "corruption."[60]

This final definition of sex as disgusting completes the patristic characterization of sex in general. All these characteristics applied to sexuality for both men and women, and defined the carnal enemy against which ascetics of both genders were fighting. However, the Fathers' recommendations for leading an ascetic life were not the same for men and women. This is because while there were general character-istics of sexuality that applied to everyone, there were also gender-specific characteristics that applied to men and women differently. The division of humanity into men and women seémed for the early Fathers to parallel the division of the world into the spiritual and the physical. Men represented the spiritual part of the world, while women repre-sented the carnal. Since men were by nature closer to the spiritual realm, the Fathers did not identify specific sexual characteristics of men, although they did discuss what it meant to be male. The nature of men's sexuality was derived from their view of what it meant to be a man and men's natural place in the social order. As the spirit was ideally supposed to govern the flesh, spiritual (or rational, as the sources some-times say) man was to govern carnal woman. Isidore of Seville summar-ized patristic wisdom when he wrote: "Women are under the power of men because they are frequently spiritually fickle. Therefore, they should be governed by the power of men."[61] Elsewhere, he refers to man as being the "head of woman."[62] These two descriptions, power and head, characterize and shape patristic views of men. Men's strength and rationality provided their justification – indeed, their obligation – to rule. These two qualities endowed men with power and conversely, then, power was the mark of a man.

Man's power could be seen in his physical qualities and bearing, which clearly marked him as different from woman. The importance of the difference between the two genders led to statements of the obvious: "... in men and women there are different customs, different complex-ion, different gestures, gait, and strength, different qualities of voice."[63] These differences marked men as being rougher and stronger than soft women. Some of men's "manly qualities," like a "rugged voice, rough speech and shaggy eyebrows,"[64] may seem rather trivial, but they visibly marked the order in a world in which spiritual power was to rule the flesh.

A man's position of power dictated a second characteristic of manliness: that he be active in the world and the active partner in his relationship with women. Patristic understanding of the different loci of sexual pleasure in men and women speaks to men's active role in sexual activity. Men's sexuality was located in the loins, while women's was in the navel.[65] The loins represented strength, musculature and activity, while the navel represented passivity, receptiveness and nurturing. In this view of sexuality, which makes a strong and necessary distinction between active and passive partner, the Church Fathers were drawing from the classical heritage which formed the background for their thought. Paul Veyne studied the sexual ideas of the Roman Empire and concluded that the Church Fathers continued the Roman perspective that "to be active was to be male, whatever the sex of the compliant partner. To take one's pleasure was virile, to accept it servile. ...."[66] What the Church Fathers did was to accept the distinction between active and passive partner, but divide the world along gender lines as well. In other words, it was no longer acceptable to be the active partner in a homosexual relationship, but it was mandatory, if one was male, to be the active partner in a heterosexual relationship. Thus, while the Fathers banned homosexual acts, even for the active partner, they seemed to accept the maxim that Veyne has articulated so well: that to take one's pleasure actively was the manly way.

It is in this context that we might understand Isidore of Seville's statement that masturbation was effeminate.[67] Isidore said that in masturbation a man dishonored the vigor of his sex by his languid body.[68] In effect, masturbation was an unmanly, servile acceptance of pleasure rather than an active taking of it. To be manly, then, was to be active, rational and powerful and through these qualities to lead. This position came with some responsibilities, of course. For example, Ambrose noted that Adam's sin was greater than Eve's, for Eve was weaker, so her fall was more understandable. Adam was the stronger, so his sin was greater.[69]

Not all the early churchmen would have agreed with Ambrose's attribution of responsibility. Since men were considered to be more spiritual than fleshly by nature, it was felt that if it were not for the temptations of women, men would be more able to avoid the sins of the flesh. In fact, the sexual characteristics I have described as belonging to man were not really considered central to his being. They merely indicate how manliness would be expressed sexually; sexuality did not define manliness. Women, on the other hand, according to the Fathers, were carnal and sexual by nature. Spiritual men in the presence of carnal women would be tempted to be drawn into the physical realm. With every act of intercourse the metaphor of the spirit trapped in the flesh was made real by spiritual man's penetration into woman's body. In some ways all the dangers of the physical world that the Fathers warned of as distracting from spiritual things were embodied in woman, and their analysis of woman's character and sexuality reveals this.

Just as for the Fathers the core of the physical realm was sex, the primary characteristic of women who belonged to the carnal world was lust, which was a manifestation of their gender. Isidore of Seville, in his *Etymologies*, revealed the degree to which women were defined by their sexuality: "... the word *femina* comes from the Greek derived from the force of fire because her concupiscence is very passionate: women are more libidinous than men."[70] It was this essential sexuality that represented a perpetual lure of the flesh for men who got near any woman, for all women were temptresses who constantly reproduced Eve's initial temptation of Adam. As Jerome warned:

> It is not the harlot, or the adulteress who is spoken of, but woman's love in general is accused of ever being insatiable; put it out, it bursts into flame; give it plenty, it is again in need; it enervates a man's mind, and engrosses all thought except for the passion which it feeds.[71]

Here Jerome not only reveals the fear of women's sexuality, but also identifies the nature of the threat. By "enervating a man's mind" and interfering with his "thought," woman removes him from the rational world of the mind that defines him as spiritual and, indeed, defines his masculinity.

For the Church Fathers, woman's lust would not have been so dangerous had it not been for the fact that her lust was related to her role as temptress. It is important to note that women were not temptresses out of desire to be so; it was just part of their nature. In fact, even if a woman did not try to tempt a man she would do so anyway, as Tertullian had noted with regard to visual lust. A woman who was seen by a man was guilty of attempting to seduce him. Ambrose, in a burst of generosity, said that a woman should not be blamed for being a temptation, for "a woman can't be blamed for being as she was born."[72] While removing the blame, however, Ambrose and others left woman in an ontological state of lustful temptress that defined her as carnal. Thus women were blamed for being what they were, rather than for anything they did. Because of this, people like Tertullian could characterize women as the "devil's gateway"[73] and suggest that women should want to wear mourning clothes all the time as penance for "the ignominy ... of original sin and the odium of being the cause of the fall of the human race."[74]

Fear of woman's sexuality and the related fear of what this would do to man's spirituality also extends to a more concrete fear of women's bodies. Fathers showed suspicion of everything from a woman's hair, "with which she had ... deceived many,"[75] to her menstrual blood, which caused "fruits not to germinate, wine to sour, plants to parch, trees to lose their fruit, iron to be corroded, bronze to turn black and dogs to become rabid if they eat anything that has come in contact with the blood."[76] The perceived power in women to corrupt not only men, but almost everything else, is remarkable and must have been quite threatening to the principle that defined maleness – that is, power.

However, the "natural order" of male dominance and power was restored by the particular nature of woman's sexuality. Her sexuality was seen as open and receptive, thus giving a metaphorical logic to a sexual role for women of passivity and submission. The metaphor of sexual women being "open" was pervasive, and this openness was extended to include such things as garrulousness – that is, women with open mouths. Tertullian gives a striking example of the degree to which women with "open mouths," or talkative, were associated with the lust that was defined in women by openness. He says of talkative women that "... their god ... is their belly, and so too what is neighbor to the belly."[77] While being open meant that women were lustful and receptive, it also labeled them as passive recipients of men's power, once men had been lured to lust through women's natural temptations. In this way, even though men had been enticed into falling from their natural spiritual state, they could retain their power and express it sexually by dominating their partner. This sexual paradigm would have been familiar to men in the Roman Empire who had grown up considering men's role as active sexually. The Church may have been forbidding men to be the active partners in homosexual relationships, but it was giving them license to remain the dominant partner in the heterosexual relationship that remained to them. Woman was supposed to "show deference, ... show she is ready to be guided."[78] A wife should wear a veil as a "yoke" to show her subjection to her husband.[79] Woman's sexuality gave her enough power to lure men into lust, but the lure brought with it its own trap: to be subjected to the husband she subjected to her flesh.

The carnal world that the Fathers saw as based on sex had its own order and logic, but as we have seen, it was an order they disdained as vastly inferior to the spiritual order that was also available to people. Those who chose the path of the carnal, even in marriage, brought their bodies down to the level of the flesh, "falling into the abyss of lust ... [and] wallowing in the mire,"[80] the "corruption [that] attaches to all intercourse."[81]

Even in this dualistic system of flesh and spirit, however, the Fathers saw the possibility of choosing the life of the spirit rather than that of the flesh. But for them the choice was neither simple nor the same for every-one. They believed that carnal women had a more difficult time follow-ing the life of the spirit than did spiritual men, so different rules must apply to women and to men. Furthermore, churchmen were faced with the problem of independent ascetics of both genders, who were violating social and ecclesiastical order by remaining outside both Church and society. To solve these problems, the Fathers had to establish a theory of celibacy that was consistent with their view of sexuality and gender, recognized the differences between men and women, and kept chaste women in the subservient roles which marked the order of the world for their married counterparts.

2

The Early Fathers on Virginity:
The Spiritual World

Historians and theologians have written volumes on virginity in the early centuries of Christianity.[1] However, most works have considered virginity as if it were unrelated to attitudes of sexuality, and this has led to an inadequate understanding of the ideal of virginity. Furthermore, it has led to an insensitive and too easy rejection of the early Fathers as misogynist, without a consideration of the opinions and fears that shaped their proclamations. Here I shall look at the spiritual world that was the mirror image of the carnal world for the early Fathers.

Since the early Fathers understood men to be primarily spiritual and women carnal, it is logical that they considered it more natural for men to aspire to and achieve a spiritual life. Men were considered holy when they exhibited the male characteristics of spirituality and power in their purest forms. Stories of the early desert fathers contain many examples of such men, whose power over their own flesh earned them the power to perform miracles of all sorts. Their sanctity emerged from their natural masculine characteristic of power. Women who aspired to be holy presented a different problem for patristic thinkers. Since by nature women were primarily carnal, in order to achieve spirituality they had to renounce those things that defined them as women. In other words, since by nature women were lustful temptresses who were open to sexuality, they could not act as women if they were to be spiritual. By choosing a spiritual life women had to reject or transcend their gender, which was by definition sexual and reproductive.

Jerome noted: "... as long as woman is for birth and children, she is different from men as body is from soul. But if she wishes to serve Christ more than the world, then she will cease to be a woman and will be called man."[2] Ambrose, too, wrestled with the question of the nature of a spiritual woman, and wrote: "... she who believes progresses to complete manhood. ... She then does without worldly name, gender of

26

body, youthful seductiveness, and garrulousness of old age."[3] In this short statement, Ambrose summarized the feminine characteristics that defined women as carnal beings: their seductiveness and openness, which included talkativeness. He further recognized that by rejecting those things which had defined their gender, they almost of necessity became different beings. This sort of logic posed a real problem for early Christian society. Jo Ann McNamara observed that at the turn of the third century, "... African churches were afire with the question of whether or not virgins were still women." If they were women, society had to be restructured to accommodate them; if they were not, they had to be admitted into the ranks of men.[4]

The potential of virgins to transcend their gender was threatening not only to a social structure that placed men at the head of women, but also to simple, observable reality. As Tertullian pointed out, "If the man is head of the woman of course [he is] of the virgin too, ... unless the virgin is a third generic class, some monstrosity with a head of its own."[5] Much of Tertullian's tract on the veiling of virgins argues that virgins belonged to a sub-category of the universal class of woman, and as such were subject to the laws that governed women.[6] Tertullian's arguments did not attack the dualistic principle that formed the basis for the problem in the first place, for he too believed that women represented the carnal world. Instead, he argued from the observable reality that virgins still appeared to be women, with all women's secondary sexual characteristics. For example, he said it was clearly ridiculous to suppose that it was the contact of man during the first sexual act that made a female a woman instead of a virgin. He said age itself turned a virgin into a woman; it was "mother nature and father time" that did it. In fact at puberty, "already her voice is changed, her limbs fully formed, ... [and] the months paying their tribute [with her menstrual flow]."[7] In fact, for the Fathers to believe that a man would be the instrument of a woman's sexual awakening would have violated the very dualist principle that defined man as spiritual and woman as carnal and created the problem of the identification of spiritual women in the first place. In any case, Tertullian concluded, for all the Fathers, that a virgin continued to be a woman even though she renounced the carnality of her sexuality, which had been the primary definition of her gender.

Nevertheless, the Fathers had to consider what it was that characterized virgins as women. By renouncing their sexuality, women had rejected most of the things that had defined their gender – their lustfulness, their role as temptresses, and the openness that was the physical definition of their sexuality. The only characteristic that remained of the original four which had defined womanhood was passivity. Therefore, the Fathers looked upon passivity as that quality which defined virgins as women, and insisted that virgins had to be compliant and subject to men just as other women were. For Tertullian this included veiling their heads to demonstrate that they were just as bound to the power of men as their married sisters.[8]

While the Fathers rejected the idea that women living a chaste life would acquire a masculine independence, they did nevertheless acknowledge that women who took vows of chastity were far better off than married women. To abstain from sexuality meant to reject the carnal world and thus to accrue all the spiritual benefits implied by such a rejection. Dumm summarized Jerome's views on the virtues of virginity, and this summary could just as easily apply to the other early Fathers: "It is the virgin who is most perfectly detached from this world ..., it is likewise the virgin who is most perfectly emancipated from sin and its bitter consequences, even from death itself."[9] The Fathers firmly believed that the ideal life was that of dedicated virginity, followed by widowhood or chaste marriage. Marriage, with its carnal debt, was of necessity the lowest in a hierarchy which drew such a strict distinction between the flesh and the spirit. Strong advocates of virginity like Jerome repeatedly had to assure their readers that by such praise of virginity they were not really denigrating marriage,[10] which would have made them liable to suspicion of heresy. In reality, their praise of marriage was pretty weak compared to their strong advocacy of the spiritual realm represented by a life of virginity.

The Fathers argued that a spiritual life would accrue many advantages for women who pursued it. The first of these advantages echoed the argument of the women themselves, who were claiming freedom as a corollary to an asexual life. The Fathers may have refused to grant virgins complete freedom from the constraints that bound women, but they did note that virgins were still freer than married women. Marriage was a "bond" and a "servitude" in which wives were subject to their husbands. Ambrose said: "The marriage bond is not then to be shunned as though it were sinful, but rather declined as being a galling burden."[11] Marriage would bind a woman not only to her husband's will, but also to difficulties inherent in a wife's role, such as "pregnancy, the crying of infants, the torture caused by a rival, the cares of household management."[12] In an age of inadequate birth control and medical care, to avoid these burdens must have seemed to grant very real personal advantages to some women.

Another personal advantage a virgin might gain was a kind of freedom from the anonymity that was the fate of most wives. Jerome wrote to Demetrias praising her choice of a chaste life: "Had you become a man's bride but one province would have known of you; while as a Christian virgin you are known to the whole world."[13] Even had she married, Demetrias would have been well known because of her important family connections. In Jerome's view, however, her vow of chastity gave her a personal notoriety for spirituality, not an acknowledgement of family ties. Perhaps not all Christian virgins could look for the kind of renown a member of a senatorial family might enjoy, but the possibility of acclaim was a very real one, for by the late fourth century stories of famous virgins were circulating throughout the Empire. These stories were not popular because women were avoiding the cares of childbirth; they were popular because such women were seen to have acquired power through the spirituality of their lives.

The spiritual power that came with a life of chastity was similar to the power martyrs achieved through their sacrifice. Virginity, too, was seen as a sacrifice, a sacrifice of sexuality and personal fecundity. By choosing a life of spirituality a virgin killed the fleshly part of her, thus becoming a martyr to the cause of spirituality. Ambrose expressed this association with martyrdom: "For virginity is not praiseworthy because it is found in martyrs, but because itself makes martyrs."[14] Just as martyrs could use their power to bring some benefit to others in the Christian community, so virgins and widows could also bring a public benefit. Virgins, by their renunciation of private fertility, were seen as symbols that could bring fertility or prosperity to the community at large. Widows who lived chaste lives were thought to have a special power of prayer, and people gave charity to widows in exchange for their prayers.[15] Since women who lived chaste lives were considered important to Christian communities, their ways of life generated considerable patristic analysis. Just as the Fathers explored the essence of the carnal realm by scrutinizing the nature of sexuality, they considered the nature of the spiritual realm by contemplating the essence of virginity.

The metaphoric structure of patristic language yields insight into Church Fathers' views on virginity. One of the principal metaphoric patterns by which they understood virginity was through images of things closed. Obviously, this was drawn from the association of sexuality with feminine openness discussed in Chapter 1. Ambrose explicitly listed metaphors for virginity so that, as he said, his readers might more easily understand its nature. He called virginity a "closed door," a "closed garden" and a "fountain."[16] Ambrose and the other Fathers drew upon the Song of Songs for the images of garden and fountain to refer to women, giving biblical authority to their visions of women.

The fountain to which Ambrose referred also represented a metaphor for something closed, just like the "door" and the "garden." This association becomes clear in another passage, where he referred to the virgin's "fountain": "let no one disturb, no one mark, and keep intact the seal you have received by nature."[17] So the fountain to which all the Fathers referred with some regularity was actually a "sealed fountain," which continued the definition of virginity as the closed opposite of women's open sexuality. Ambrose elaborated on the image of the closed fountain by explaining that such a fountain would serve only "pure liquids"[18] since it was untainted by sexuality and corruption. The metaphoric wisdom implied by this statement paralleled prevailing medical opinion that it would be possible to distinguish a virgin from a married woman by a urinalysis, for a virgin's urine would be clear instead of cloudy like the urine of a woman who had intercourse with a man.[19] In the patristic view – and in this case in the medical view as well – a fall from purity would lead literally to a fall from purity with regard to bodily fluids, showing once again that the body itself could become transformed into a more fleshly or spiritual entity.

Literal application of metaphors pervades patristic thought, and the recognition of this fact helps us to understand one of Ambrose's letters on the subject of an allegedly fallen virgin. Ambrose wrote to a bishop reprimanding the prelate for his treatment of a case of a dedicated virgin who was brought before him accused (with little evidence) of breaking her vow of chastity. Despairing of sorting out the accusations and denials, the Bishop called a midwife to inspect the maiden and resolve the question. Ambrose was against this resolution, and he gave several reasons for his disapproval. First of all he said, rather practically, that midwives could not always tell from a physical inspection whether or not the hymen had been ruptured. Furthermore, an incompetent midwife might break the hymen, perhaps violating an innocent woman. Finally, Ambrose said it set an unacceptable precedent that might advocate periodic inspections of virgins to check on the fulfillment of their vows.[20] Underlying these explanations, however, was Ambrose's sense of outrage that the virgin had been "opened" for inspection, thus violating her metaphoric integrity if not her physical integrity. He argued that the inspection "prostitutes the other's modesty"[21] – which, of course, it did, given the strong association of virginity with being closed.

Ambrose's practical and patient solution to the dilemma of how to tell whether a virgin was lying about her intactness was simply to wait. He said that eventually pregnancy would reveal her crime to the world in a way that would permit no dispute. One might wonder how Ambrose's solution would trap a woman whose fall had been brief and safe, but since he believed that sexuality, and particularly woman's sexuality, was habit-forming, he probably assumed that one indiscretion would lead to another, finally arriving at the damning pregnancy. In any case, this example shows not only the dramatic association between virginity and being closed but also that patristic reflections on the nature of virginity and sexuality yielded practical applications as they worked to create a society that encompassed the celibate as well as the married.

Since it was important that virgins should live out the predominant metaphor of female spirituality, that of being closed, the Fathers were careful to articulate in which ways women might be "open" without slipping into carnality. I have already explained that ears seemed to be exempt from the danger of carnality, and Ambrose added the mind to the ears as one of the safe things for virgins to keep open. Since the ears were kept open to be educated in the ways of God, an open and receptive mind must necessarily follow. The last permissible "open" bodily part was the hands, so that the virgin who was divesting herself of worldly cares might also free herself of money which might bind her to worldly affairs. Ambrose summarized these permissibly open qualities while at the same time reminding virgins of their first responsibility: to keep their spirituality enclosed:

> Listen, virgin, diligently open your ears and keep your modesty closed; open your hands that you recognize paupers; close your door so dishonor doesn't creep in; open your mind and keep pure.[22]

An enclosed spirituality provided a direct contrast with the open sexuality that characterized patristic understanding of womanhood. This contrast demonstrates the degree to which views on virginity were derived directly from views on sexuality, and one can continue to follow this relationship through patristic reflections on fertility. Sexuality had brought with it one particular fruit, children. Therefore spirituality, too, had to bear fruits, albeit spiritual rather than fleshly ones, and the next category of metaphors by which the Fathers understood virginity were metaphors of fertility.

Individual virgins were metaphorically like Christ's chaste Bride, the Church, and also like the Virgin Mary. The Church was seen as a fruitful Bride[23] bringing forth faithful congregations of children; and Mary, of course, was the perfect fruitful Virgin in whose womb the Incarnation was born. Similarly, the individual bride of Christ was spiritually fruitful, and this fecundity was described in terms as physical as the descriptions of childbirth for those in a carnal union. Ambrose said: "... immaculately your faith will be born and your piety exposed; that in your uterus you will receive the Holy Spirit and bring forth the spirit of God."[24]

The spiritual fruits that would be born from virgin flesh were not easy to see or describe. This difficulty perhaps posed a particular problem during the late Empire, when declining populations seemed to make women who took vows of chastity a luxury the body politic could ill afford. Ambrose addressed these critics using a quasi-demographic argument that showed a singular unconcern for a logic of cause and effect: "If anyone imagines that the human race is decreasing because of vows of virginity he should consider this: a small number of virgins means a low population. It is a fact that the population is highest where a commitment to virginity is strongest."[25] The examples of these areas of high population to which Ambrose referred were Alexandria and North Africa. In fact, the argument would more accurately be stated by saying that areas of high population could be counted on to produce more actual numbers of women willing to take vows of virginity than areas of low population. However, Ambrose did not concern himself with producing a ratio of virgins to total women. He did not need mathematical accuracy to demonstrate what he knew to be true – that virgins were associated with fertility.

It is not an easy task to work one's way through patristic metaphoric language in order to understand exactly in which ways the Fathers saw virgins as fertile. Ambrose's statement notwithstanding, I am sure the Fathers did not see virginity as a mechanism for promoting a population explosion. In fact, it appears that the fruits of virginity were the virgins themselves; the brides of Christ, by their spiritual marriages, gave birth to their spiritual selves. Presumably, they also served as examples to inspire other virgins, but the metaphors of virginity do not really lend themselves to such practical interpretations. The virgins were like the Virgin Mary, bride and mother in one person, and as such they were self-sufficient and complete in themselves.[26] Thus, by preserving their virginity, these women were reborn spiritually and therefore spiritually fecund. In this context the popular nature metaphors for virgins become comprehensible. They were described as flowers of the Church,[27] lilies,[28] shoots in full bloom,[29] and grapes of a vineyard.[30] As they reproduced the spiritual life, spirituality bloomed in them and they crowned the earthly Church with garlands of virginity to provide a contrast to the physical children who were born of earthly marriages and populated the Church. Virgins were the living examples of the spiritual realm on earth.

The spiritual life was not easy to attain, however, and Church Fathers spent a good deal of time discussing how women could actually achieve the ideal they were advocating. A virgin's way of life was as important to the Fathers as her initial commitment to chastity, since they felt that it was possible to "... be a virgin in body and not in spirit."[31] Their prescriptions for how virgins should live are covered in much detail in many of their writings. Here I shall show how many of these prescriptions are derived directly from their view of sex.

Once a woman had made up her mind not to marry carnally, she was supposed to make a public profession to that effect. The requirement of a public profession appeared as early as c. 300 AD in Spain at the Council of Elvira, which required women to make a public "pact of virginity."[32]

Jerome, too, seems to have advocated a public ceremony by describing an ideal profession in his letter to Demetrias. According to Jerome, a virgin was to appear before her bishop, who would cover her head with a bridal veil and say: "I wish to present you ... as a chaste virgin to Christ." The woman would respond: "The king hath brought me into his chambers." The woman's companions would bear public witness to the spiritual marriage, saying: "The king's daughter is all glorious within."[33] The public aspect of the profession is important because it provides a way for the Church to identify and control women who were choosing to dedicate themselves to God.

The phrase in the profession, as described by Jerome, that referred to a woman entering the king's chambers points to the way of life Jerome thought she could expect. She was no longer to move about freely in the world. The chaste bride of Christ was to avoid worldly society; she was to "... avoid the market place and the city squares,"[34] attend no weddings,[35] visit no married ladies or widows who had not taken vows of chastity,[36] and certainly she was not to travel to "visit the daughters of a strange land."[37] Ideally her world was to be restricted to her chamber, where she would serve Christ. As Jerome warned her, "Do not seek the Bridegroom in the streets ...stay home with [Him]."[38] In these statements we see the beginnings of the requirement for enclosure of nuns, but this requirement grew out of a deeply felt, yet barely articulated, association of women's sexuality with openness. If a sexual woman were open to the world, a virgin had to be closed to it and from it, or how could she be really spiritual? Essentially a virgin, by remaining enclosed in her house, was living the metaphor of her closed body. Ambrose expressed this sexual association: "what is more excellent (especially in a maiden whose private parts demand modesty) than ... retirement?"[39] Just as her sexual parts were to be hidden, so was she if she were to remain non-sexual.

The Fathers associated enclosure with modesty, for as we have seen, they associated being visible with participating in a lustful act. Tertullian said that physical virginity was not enough; a woman needed modesty as well.[40] Ambrose took this logic to its fullest extent, saying that without modesty virginity did not even exist.[41] Virginity could be violated by a lustful look that would offend the virgin's heavenly Bridegroom. Jerome warned: "Jesus is jealous. He does not choose that your face should be seen of others."[42]

The ideal virgin, then, spent most of her time indoors. However, occasionally she could go out in the world – for example, to attend church. At these times, she was to take her enclosure with her by keeping herself heavily veiled to avoid jeopardizing her virginity by seeing and being seen. Again the association between veiling, a form of enclosure, and sexuality emerges from the texts: "Let her whose lower parts are not bare have her upper likewise covered."[43] Tertullian was so adamant that he was led to state, rather extremely, "[When] you have denuded a maiden in regard to her head, ... forthwith she wholly ceases to be a virgin to herself; she has undergone a change."[44] A virgin's manner of dress, then, was critical to her profession. Not only was she to be veiled, but obviously she was to avoid ostentatious displays of style and wealth.[45] More than that, however, she was also to avoid ostentatious asceticism, for such extremities in dress would call attention to the woman, causing "... men to point their fingers. ..."[46] Such attention would violate the requirement of non-visible modesty which was a patristic stipulation for a virgin life. In sum, our virgin would go out in public as little as possible, and when she did she would dress moderately and modestly. Ideally she would not be noticed, but if she were, all would know that she was a modest, dedicated virgin.[47]

While the Fathers argued vehemently that a woman should stay enclosed in order to remain spiritual, they recognized that it was not always desirable for her to be totally alone. Jerome noted that even male hermits were sometimes subject to excesses which might lead them to heterodoxy. "Now if this is true of men," he continued, "how much more does it apply to women whose fickle and vacillating minds, if left to their own devices, soon degenerate."[48] Once the Fathers had demonstrated that virgins were women, they argued that virgins, like other women, should not live independently or alone. The perfect virgin was not to enclose herself completely alone with Christ and her prayers; she was to live in a community with other similar women, dedicated virgins or widows.[49]

While living in a community, a virgin should subject herself in obedience to women who were her spiritual elders.[50] In this way, she could retain her womanly characteristics of passivity and obedience. As worldly women were to obey their husbands, so a virgin was to obey the wishes of her heavenly Spouse in the person of His representatives, the head of the community of women and the local bishop. When Jerome referred to communities of women, he was using the term broadly and informally. During the fourth century there were few formal "communities" of holy women in the West, and certainly none as complex as the ascetics' foundations in the East. However, Jerome used the term to refer to women living in their homes, but surrounded by a like-minded "community" of women which could provide guidance and direction. The recommendations in Jerome's letters were used later to provide guidance for formal monastic communities of women.[51]

The Fathers believed that by remaining obedient, an ideal virgin would avoid taking pride in her chosen role. They repeatedly cautioned her to be humble and avoid a "passion for vainglory."[52] It was under-standable that a young virgin might be proud of her special position as one of the flowers of the Church, but Jerome warned her: "... you are destined to produce perfect fruit if only you will humble yourself under the mighty hand of God. ..."[53] She was to be a humble bride of Christ, as her sisters were humble brides of men.

While she was living obediently under some guidance, a virgin had patristic suggestions to shape most aspects of her daily life. To begin with, in accordance with patristic associations of food with sex, a virgin must severely curtail her diet. She was to fast daily, never filling her stomach,[54] and the foods she ate had to be "cooling" ones like vege-tables and mild herbs.[55] Wine was to be avoided like "poison," for it had such heating properties.[56] Water was the safest beverage, for "by nature of all drinks [it is] the most cooling."[57] So greatly did the Fathers fear the influence of food in generating sexuality that Jerome hoped his prohibitions would be followed to the extent that all the virgin's companions in the community would "be women pale and thin from fasting."[58]

Of course, since the Fathers were prohibiting anything sensual (and thus carnal), a dedicated virgin should not bathe, even in the company of other virgins. Not only might a bath heat the blood,[59] but it would violate a virgin's modesty, which the Fathers considered central to her life. Furthermore, a bath might be an indication of a maiden's pride in her appearance, and that was unacceptable, for the perfect virgin, "... by a deliberate squalor ... makes haste to spoil her natural good looks."[60] So baths joined large meals in the list of things forbidden to virgins.

As virgins were to be aloof from worldly things (like food and baths) they were also to be indifferent to personal property, even if they had once been wealthy. In fact, with their marriage to Christ their property was no longer their own, but belonged to their Husband.[61] They should use their Bridegroom's funds to do His work, giving alms to the poor, feeding the hungry and supporting communities of virgins.[62] Of course, an ideal virgin would not manage these funds herself, since she was to stay indoors and distant from the world. She should turn over her money to the Church to be managed for Christ's work.

Along with these lists of prohibited conduct, the Fathers also estab-lished a recommended program of activities for the women within celibate households. As the Fathers believed that spiritual and carnal activities could not coexist, they recommended that a virgin fill her time with spiritual activities. Jerome accented study as an excellent pastime that would replace carnal passion with a passion for learning.[63] He urged Eustochium to "read often, learn all that you can."[64] He recommended the reading of Scripture and of Church Fathers like Cyprian, Athanasius and Hilary.[65] All this study should not lead to pride, however, or to a woman exhibiting her knowledge in disputation. She should "not seek to appear over-eloquent"[66] but use her knowledge for private spiritual edification.

In addition to study, a virgin should pray often. Jerome recommended the daily cycle of prayers at the third, sixth, and ninth hours as well as evening, midnight, and dawn.[67] Ambrose's recommendations of prayer were not quite as precise, but they were certainly as frequent. He recommended prayer before and after eating, when getting up and when going to bed. He also suggested that a virgin should repeat the Creed often during the day, and when alone at night in her chamber she should meditate continually on Christ.[68]

Finally, in any time that remained during the day, a virgin should take up her womanly occupations of spinning, weaving or "rolling up yarn others have spun."[69] The virgin's day was to be full of activities that would keep her from descending to the carnal realm. Her life was busy and spiritually productive, leading Ambrose to observe a similarity between the virgin and the bee: "virginity is fit to be compared to bees, so laborious is it, so modest, so continent. The bee feeds on dew, knows no marriage couch ...," and the dew upon which the bee fed was the Divine Word which would sustain the virgin in her spirituality.[70]

However, it was not enough simply to do all these tasks. They had to be performed with the correct bearing and in the correct spirit, or they would not contribute to the virgin's spirituality. The first requirement for the virgin's conduct in her daily life was that she be silent. This requirement for silence again grows from the association between openness and sexuality. The Fathers felt that a mouth open in speech revealed a woman open to the world. Speech was also an active, not a passive, act, thus considered unfeminine. Therefore, virgins who must be non-sexual must also be silent. Ambrose equated silence with modesty, and said that virginity required both.[71] The association between silence and modesty makes most sense when one understands the strong sexual context of the prohibition. Ambrose warned: "your mouth should neither open easily nor respond to every commonplace address. ... Speak to Christ alone.[72] ... For in truth in much speaking there is abundance of sin."[73] The requirements of silence as well as enclosure have often been looked upon as misogynist impulses, and they certainly may have had such consequences for the women who lived by these strict rules. The origin of the thought, however, lay in a fear of sexuality on the part of the Fathers, who held such a fundamentally dualistic view of the world. They feared sexuality for women as well, and these prohibitions were designed to "save" the virgins from their own carnal nature, which was seen as open.

If she adhered to all these rules, a virgin might hope to accomplish a spiritual life. This still was not guaranteed, for the Fathers were careful to downplay the importance of strictly physical integrity, or the avoidance of sexual intercourse. As we have seen from their prohibitions, true virginity (or spirituality) could be lost by indulging in food, pride, a glance, or any number of other hazards. Even if a virgin avoided all these, however, there remained one more hurdle: she had to keep even her thoughts pure. Ambrose said: "Note that mere physical virginity does not gain merit, but rather, the integrity of the mind."[74] Jerome warned: "virginity may be lost even by a thought."[75]

The difficulties involved in the way of life of the ideal dedicated virgin emerge vividly in the patristic works. The life as prescribed by the Fathers is sparse and hard and full of hazards. According to them, even a thought could render all for naught. Yet the rewards were comparably large. The virgin could expect to be blessed with eternal life, as Jerome said: "... the end of marriage is death, but the compensating fruit of sanctification, fruit belonging either to virginity or to continence, is eternal life."[76] Virgins did not have to wait for death to reap the benefits of their spirituality. Their bodies were redeemed from carnality, and in a sense they experienced a resurrection of the flesh while still alive. Their bodies became the temples of God.[77]

It is difficult for us to grasp the degree to which the Fathers believed that the virgin's body was spiritualized while remaining physical. The strongest example of this is the story of Thecla, as told by Ambrose, who related this story to demonstrate the power of virgin flesh. Thecla was arrested and sent to be eaten by a fierce lion who had been starved for many days. As the lion charged at her, Thecla, "avoiding the gaze of men, ... offered her vital parts to the fierce lion." The lion was awed by her exposure and lay down and licked her feet. Ambrose explained that "it could not injure the sacred body of a virgin. ... Virginity has in itself so much that is admirable, that even lions admire it."[78] The path to spirituality as outlined by the Fathers was hard, but the resulting holiness was so physical, so obvious, that even animals recognized it. The striking contrast between the spiritual and the carnal realms was visible to all.

The lifestyle for chaste women recommended by the Fathers bears little resemblance to the independence of Ecdicia, or to the freedom claimed by women under the ascetic tradition that had come from the East. The early Fathers had a profound fear of sexuality that might draw them from spirituality, and an intense fear of women, in whom they thought sexuality resided. Therefore they thought to save both men and women from temptation by controlling women who might wish to be spiritual by having them live enclosed, silent and obedient lives. This was the only way the Fathers believed virgins could avoid the open sexuality of women who participated fully in the carnal world. The patristic view of sexuality and its resulting influence on their recommendations for behavior pervaded Christian thought and, by extension, Western thought. Their view of sex remains our burden as well as that of the women (and, indeed, men) who lived it. However, this is not the only patristic tradition that comes to us. Even more influential is the thought of St Augustine, the greatest of the Western Fathers. Augustine rejected the dualism implicit in the early Fathers and established a different vision of sexuality and of virginity, neither of which would yield the freedom for women claimed by ascetics.

3

Augustine's Sexual Revolution

The early Fathers may have thought they had established a Christian view of sexuality and articulated its place in a Christian life, but theirs was neither the last word on the subject, nor the most influential. Augustine, the Latin Father whose influential hand would guide future Christian thinkers, dramatically changed Christian views of sexuality and its mirror image, virginity. For Augustine, sexuality was not an imperfection, an accident brought into being by Adam's and Eve's sin, but a part of God's plan. Furthermore, unlike the early Fathers, Augustine did not see sexuality as a primarily female quality, a part of woman's mysterious earthiness, but believed sexuality was demonstrated and defined by an erection, the mark of male lust.[1] However, Augustine's revolutionary transformation of early patristic views of sexuality neither redeemed sexual intercourse from condemnation nor freed women from the burden of sexual shame. The origins of Augustine's rejection of the early Fathers' dualism, as well as his own discomfort with the flesh, may be found in his youthful attraction to Manichaeism.

Because of this early adherence to Manichaeism, Augustine began his religious life with an even more profoundly dualistic view of the world than did the early Fathers. With his conversion from heresy and his Christian baptism in 387, Augustine was vigorous in setting aside and guarding against elements of dualism. After his conversion, however, he had to wrestle with the question of human sexuality in a Christian context just as the early Fathers had done. He himself recognized the importance of the "question of the procreation of offspring before man merited death by sinning ..." and the significance of "the coition of mortal bodies. ..."[2] For Augustine, however, these questions were considered against the background of Manichaean dualism that he was rejecting. Because of this, he introduced a way of understanding sexual-

ity that departed from that of the early Fathers, whose subtle, if orthodox, dualism was unacceptable to him.

Like the early Fathers, however, Augustine began his reflections on
the subject of sexuality by observing those who had denied it and lived
chaste lives. In his early tract *The Catholic and Manichaean Ways of Life*
– written in 388, the year after his baptism – Augustine described
women who lived ascetic lives in the desert, and women who lived in
communities in urban areas like Rome. He made a point of noting that
although they might seem to be like Manichaeans in their rejection of
sexuality and in their fasts, they were significantly different. He argued
that these Christian holy women were not rejecting the flesh, they were
subsuming all their austerities under Christian charity.[3] Love, not abstinence, marked the Christian ascetic for Augustine. Here he began his
departure from Fathers like Jerome, who had stressed physical renunciation. Jerome might have said their austerity ruled their charity, rather
than the other way around. However, the early Fathers did recognize, as
did Augustine, that Christian celibates had to distinguish themselves
from others who were practicing sexual abstinence. Augustine said that
Manichaeans who practiced continence in the wrong spirit were not
practicing continence at all.[4]

The Bishop continued his vindication of Christian asceticism against
charges of Manichaeism in his important tract "Reply to Faustus the
Manichaean," written about 400. In this work he elaborated his
arguments and began to advance the view that the genital organs and
sexuality were God-given, and therefore positive.[5] He continued the
development of his anti-Manichaean thought on marriage and sexuality
when he came to the defense of Christian marriage in "The Good of
Marriage," which he wrote upon entering the debate between Jerome
and Jovinian. He thought Jerome's response to Jovinian had been too
close to Manichaeism for comfort.[6]

In these early anti-Manichaean reflections, Augustine was beginning
nothing less than a vindication of sexuality. The early Fathers had seen
sexual intercourse as an evil in a fallen Christian world, but Augustine
saw sexual intercourse as a part of God's plan, a "good." He said that
God had provided "goods" to satisfy people's "natural needs." Such
needs were wisdom, to be satisfied by the good of learning; health, to be
satisfied by the goods of food, drink and sleep; and friendship, to be
satisfied by marriage and sexual intercourse.[7] Sexual intercourse, then,
was moved into the same category of benefit as learning. The early
Fathers would never have done this, seeing the latter as spiritual, therefore good, and the former as carnal, therefore evil. Augustine's rejection
of Manichaeism led him to reject any idea that the flesh, or indeed
carnal things, could be evil: "Actually, these two are both goods; spirit is

a good and the flesh is a good. And man, who consists of both, ruling one and serving the other, is indeed a good. ...."[8]

The evolution of Augustine's thought about sexuality was given further impetus in about 412 during his dialogue against the Pelagians, who raised the question of how original sin was passed from parent to child.[9] Out of these debates Augustine further developed views on sexuality, reproduction, and marriage that became increasingly articulated first in the *City of God*, begun about 413, then in his tracts written in response to the Pelagian criticism of Julian of Eclanum. This debate generated his writings "On Marriage and Concupiscence," "On Adulterous Marriage," and finally his long works *Against Julian*, all written between 419 and 421.[10]

By all these writings which dealt with sexual intercourse, Augustine was trying to change Christian understanding of sexuality, but he recognized that an anti-sexual context already existed in Christian thought, and he was no stranger to the strong belief that sexuality was at best a distraction from piety. To achieve any vindication of sexuality Augustine had to explain, for example, such established practices as the necessity for purification after intercourse, nocturnal emissions or women's menstrual periods. If all these occurrences were natural and part of God's plan, then why would a person need to be purified afterwards? Augustine explained that people needed purification after intercourse not because it was a sin but because during intercourse semen was expelled, and sperm is a "material shapelessness," representing only the potential for a shaped and orderly life. The sperm, then, in its "shapelessness," was a further representation – in fact a microcosm – of a "life shapeless and uninstructed," which ritual purification would order. Therefore, after any "loss of seed" men were to reassert the need for an ordered life over the formlessness represented by the sperm. It was for this same reason that Augustine said men were required to purify themselves after nocturnal emissions, not because it was a sin but because it represented the chaos against which Christians struggled.[11]

Similarly, Augustine argued that women's menstrual flow was comparable to men's loss of seed. Therefore, women needed to be purified after menstruating not because there was sin involved in this natural function, but because the "formless flow" represented a "mind without the force of discipline, unseemly fluid and dissipated. ...." The purification reasserted that a woman – and, indeed, society as a whole – preferred order over chaos, however natural such formlessness might be.[12]

It is unlikely that the average Christian followed Augustine's complex reasoning about the symbolic nature of formless matter with regard to purification after intercourse. Probably, most felt that the purification was required because sex was sinful at least to the degree that the early Fathers believed it so; sex was a victory, however temporary, of the carnal over the spiritual. Augustine's reasoning is particularly significant inasmuch as it represents the degree to which he was attempting to vindicate sexuality and remove it from the fundamentally dualistic perception that reigned in the early Church. However, to complete this task Augustine had to reconsider the nature of original sin itself.

As we have seen, the early Fathers saw the Fall as sexual: Adam and Eve sinned in the flesh and were therefore cast out of the Garden. Jerome had dismissed the possible argument that since God had created two sexes, He had intended them to come together sexually. Jerome argued that since we cannot know what was in God's mind, we can judge only on the basis of the evidence, and that evidence was that while in Paradise, Adam and Eve were virgins, and "when they were expelled they were married."[13] Augustine, on the other hand, in his exoneration of sexual intercourse, began with an argument that Jerome had dismissed. Augustine said there would have been blameless coitus in Paradise, for God had created man and woman in such a way as to make that possible. Adam's and Eve's sin was, rather, in not waiting for God to lift the prohibition on the forbidden fruit of sexuality. Therefore, the primary sin in Augustine's view was not sex, but disobedience; the "evil will preceded the evil act."[14] By their "evil will" Adam and Eve presumed to disobey God's will, and by this presumption they fell into the sin of pride. It was their pride that led them to disobey and have intercourse before God granted them permission to do so. In this way Augustine left sex as the turning point of the Fall, but he deemphasized it by placing the related sins of pride and disobedience before the action of coitus.[15]

Although Augustine deemphasized sex as the primary sin of the Fall, that does not mean he did not see sex intimately related to the Fall of humanity, for he certainly did. Sexual intercourse was the act that made manifest the disobedient will. Therefore, Augustine believed that the consequences of the Fall were sexual. Since Adam and Eve had disobeyed God, their bodies would no longer obey their wills. While there is a general inability to control many bodily experiences – such as old age, pain and, of course, death[16] – the most immediate consequence is the inability to control one's sexual organs. In Augustine's words: "For in its disobedience, which subjected the sexual organs solely to its own impulses and snatched them from the will's authority, we see a proof of the retribution imposed on man for that first disobedience."[17] In this argument is an unrelenting logic of the punishment fitting the sexual crime. By this law, women were to bear children in pain because they could not control the womb to instruct it to open and permit the child to descend painlessly.[18] Men, too, were to be punished for Adam's disobedience. A man's sexual organ also no longer served his will, but acted on an impulse all its own. As Augustine wrote: "Sometimes the impulse is an unwanted intruder, sometimes it abandons the eager lover, and desire cools off in the body while it is at boiling heat in the mind."[19]

The Fall, then, introduced disobedient flesh to disobedient humanity, and Augustine defined this disobedience of the flesh as lust.[20] Since for Augustine lust was brought into being at the Fall – unlike the early Fathers, who saw sex introduced at the Fall – Augustine vindicated sexuality, but lust or passion remained unnatural. And if lust, not sexuality, was the primary evil, Augustine departed from the early Fathers, who were preoccupied with the nature of sexuality itself. The Bishop of Hippo wanted to understand the nature of lust, not sex. As part of his considerations of the nature of it, he wrote generally about it, identifying it as the "... evil [that] ... had its origin and was transmitted through the disobedience of one man. ..."[21] This evil that was introduced at the Fall was a "disease"[22] and a "wound which can be healed [only] when [man] is reborn."[23]

These general statements about lust did not answer for Augustine the question of what was the locus – or rather, the physical expression – of it. The early Fathers looked for the location of the carnal world, and found it in woman. Augustine was not thinking in terms of the early patristic dichotomy. He was not looking for sexuality, he was looking for lust, and found it primarily – and for him most disturbingly – in the male erection: "[T]he genital organs have become ... the private property of lust. ..."[24] Augustine's embarrassment at the stirring of lust were first articulated in the *Confessions*. The young Augustine was taken to the public bath by his father, who was proud to see "the signs of active virility coming to life" in his son. His father's pride was canceled by his mother's distress at the incident,[25] and the youth was clearly troubled by his body's unwilled movement which caused yet one more incidence of disharmony between his parents. Concern for out-of-control lust pervades his *Confessions* through his famous conversion, in which God granted him the grace of chastity. But his conversion did not end his preoccupation with the physical manifestation of male lust.

In his later writings, when he repeatedly referred to the struggle to restrain passion, the images he used evoked specifically male lust. For example: "... let not concupiscence usurp for itself our members ... that they might not be instruments of iniquity unto sin. ..."[26] Furthermore, Augustine explained that to gird the loins meant to "restrain lustful appetites,"[27] but in a somewhat poignant recollection of the young Augustine's embarrassment in the bath, the Bishop wrote: "Even though it [lust] is restrained, it still moves. ..."[28] Finally, Augustine expressed himself in the biblical phrase that he repeatedly used to explain the physical expression of lust: "the law in our members fights with the law of our mind."[29]

In his old age, Augustine had to return to the problem of sexuality and present the fullest expression of his position. The Pelagians, particularly Julian of Eclanum, said that by affirming original sin, Augustine was condemning marriage. The Bishop wrote his tract "On Marriage and Concupiscence" to begin to address that charge. Finally, in 421, Augustine wrote *Against Julian* to refute the Pelagian charges as well as to refute Julian's charge that his position on sexuality was Manichaean.[30] Julian's charge of Manichaeism must have been particularly galling to Augustine, since he had spent a good deal of effort vindicating sexuality from even the limited dualism of the early Christians. Elizabeth Clark interestingly shows us that Julian had a point, for Augustine's identification of the male seed as corrupted with original sin bears some resemblance to Manichaean myths which locate man's trapped goodness in seed.[31] In spite of some similarity between Augustine's and the Manichaean biological explanations, the Bishop vehemently, and quite rightly, denied Julian's misunderstanding of his larger position: "I have never censured the union of the two sexes. ..." Augustine said that children are born with original sin not because the intercourse that produced them was sinful, but because it is impossible to have sexual intercourse without lust after the Fall, and lust is evil: "[T]he action [intercourse] is not performed without evil [lust], and this is why the children must be regenerated. ..."[32] Here, in the final articulation of his position, Augustine once again firmly placed the sin in the lust, not in the sexual act itself.

Just as in this tract Augustine argued most strongly that lust was the sin that burdened man, he also expressed most strongly his disapproval of – indeed, almost disgust at – erections, the physical expression of the sin of lust. For example, he described passion as that which "... rises up against the soul's decision in disorderly and ugly movements. ..."[33] Elsewhere Augustine described "that bestial movement"[34] against which "modesty would have to struggle."[35] The shameful erections that came about after Adam's sin of disobedience required man to clothe himself. After the Fall, embarrassment arose "from those members after sin ... [because] there was an unseemly movement there. ..."[36]

The degree to which Augustine identified the sin of lust with the male erection led Julian to ask why women covered themselves even though they had no erections to hide. Augustine responded in a way that showed a disregard for and no particular awareness of female sexuality: "It was not a visible movement the woman covered, when, in the same members, she sensed something hidden but comparable to what the man sensed. ..."[37] By focusing on an erection as the sign of lust, Augustine was forced to argue that women felt something comparable internally rather than see female sexuality as distinct from the male's, as did the early Fathers. The early Fathers saw women as sexually open to men's sexual power; Augustine saw in women an internal version of man's sexuality. Augustine did provide another reason for women covering their genitals – the sight of them might arouse lust.[38] This reason, however, was always secondary to the principal one: that man had to hide the evidence of his losing struggle with willful flesh.

Taking the logic of the foregoing argument, Augustine would seem to be placed in the unusual position of maintaining that sex is good but erections are bad. This seeming paradox is exactly Augustine's position. He says that the "unseemly movement ... would not have existed in marriage if men had not sinned."[39] He conceded that since the Fall it is impossible to have sex without lust and its physical manifestation, erections, but before the Fall it would have been possible.[40] Augustine described soft tissues that we can move by our will: the mouth, face and lungs. Therefore, it would have been possible for man to move his soft penis at will had Adam not disobeyed God's will.[41] Augustine, then, seems to be arguing that there would have been lustless, soft erections in Paradise, generated at will and capable of intercourse without destroying the woman's virginity. Julian mocked this position: "The opinion holding that in Paradise reproductive members could have obeyed the command of the will is soft and effeminate."[42] Given the late Roman association of manliness with power and dominance, Julian was probably expressing the opinion of many men had they followed Augustine's argument closely. Augustine's response was not very direct. He began by saying that the soul's power over lust is not effeminate. Here he reidentified masculinity with power, but only spiritual power. Augustine continued by saying that he would not argue over the "absence or presence of lust in Paradise"; instead he reprimanded Julian for attempting to vindicate lust.[43]

Julian would have done better to attack the early Fathers for their position on sexuality. They said there would have been no sexual intercourse in Paradise because sexuality belonged to the carnal world, which had nothing to do with the spiritual one. Augustine, on the other hand, had vindicated sexuality and made it a natural part of God's plan; on this argument sexual intercourse had a place in Paradise. For Augustine the only evil in sexuality was the evil of lust, or passion, which he was able to separate from people, bodies and even intercourse itself. Augustine may have made sexual intercourse a legitimate part of the human experience, but it would be a long time before passion was accepted as a legitimate expression of human emotion.

Once Augustine had vindicated sexual intercourse as a natural "good," the major question for him was not to understand the characteristics of sexuality as it had been for the early Fathers but to distinguish between good and bad sex – or rather, between sexuality used well or used badly. Ideal sexual intercourse could have taken place only before the Fall, before human disobedience had called forth lust. In Paradise, "They would not have had the activity of turbulent lust in their flesh ... but only the movement of peaceful will by which we command the other members of the body."[44] In prelapsarian intercourse, Augustine thought, "The man would have sowed the seed and the woman would have conceived the child when their sexual organs had been aroused by will ... and had not been excited by lust."[45] By using the word "will" in this context, Augustine was not referring to the sort of willfulness that he saw as leading to pride and sin. Instead he was associating will with reason, the faculty of mind with which he opposed passion. This association was made explicit in another passage in which he wrote that the sexual organs "... would be servants of the mind. ... They would begin their activity at the bidding of the will, instead of being stirred up by the foment of lust."[46] So, once a man had rationally decided to father a child he would have approached his wife and, in Augustine's words, "... without feeling the allurement of passion goading him on, the husband would have relaxed on his wife's bosom in tranquility of mind. ...," and the wife would be impregnated without losing her virginity, for without passion, "... the seed could be injected through the same passage by which the [menstrual] flux is ejected."[47] In this way, the conception of all children would have resembled that of Jesus, whose "... holy conception in the Virgin's womb [was] effected not through burning concupiscence of the flesh, but through ardent charity of faith. ..."[48] By such lustless conception, everyone would have avoided the burden of original sin and the burden of lust that came with it.

Since this ideal intercourse could not exist after the Fall, people had to do the best they could to approach the ideal. Marriage provided the structure for virtuous sex outside Paradise. Augustine believed that marriage was instituted by God to satisfy people's need for companionship. He saw the tie between man and wife as the "first natural tie of human society,"[49] and marriage provided an institution for "... the natural companionship between the two sexes."[50] The natural and divinely ordained institution of marriage brought three specific benefits to the partners: offspring, fidelity and sacrament.[51] By sacrament Augustine was referring to the indissolubility of the bond – for example, not putting aside a barren wife.[52] The first two benefits provided ways for men and women to use the lust with which they were born in a way that would not be sinful. As Augustine put it, "... the good and right use of passion is not passion."[53]

The first benefit of marriage was offspring. Through the positive benefit of children, marriage converted the "evil of lust" into a "good."[54] The purpose for sex in the Garden of Eden would have been to generate children; therefore the closer one could come to having intercourse only for the sake of procreation, the better off one would be. Such intercourse was presumed to be governed less by passion than by the mind's judgement. Augustine disapproved of birth control methods as "unlawful and shameful"[55] because, he said, "intercourse that goes beyond this necessity [for reproduction] no longer obeys reason but passion."[56] It is likely that in his strong renunciation of birth control, Augustine was again renouncing his Manichaean past, for the Manichaeans practiced various forms of birth control,[57] and Peter Brown suggests that the youthful Augustine and his concubine probably used birth control.[58] By having intercourse only for reproduction, Christians were further defining themselves apart from dualists. The reproductive good of marriage was to help bring the evil of lust under at least the partial control of reason, passion's opposite. The application of this principle can perhaps best be seen in the recommendations of Pope Gregory the Great at the end of the sixth century. When asked whether a man could receive communion after having intercourse, Gregory responded that he could use his own judgement and approach the altar only if he "... approaches his wife, not carried away by lustful desire but only for the sake of getting children. ..."[59]

Despite the blamelessness of purely procreative conjugal sex, Augustine recognized that, given the force of lust in fallen humanity, this kind of intercourse would not always be practiced. The second benefit of marriage, fidelity, would redeem those sexual moments that did not result in conception. Augustine noted that there was a second reason for sex in marriage in addition to procreating children. He said it was for "mutual service, ... of sustaining each other's weaknesses." In effect, conjugal intercourse would satisfy each partner's lust so that neither would fall into the temptation of adultery.[60] Indeed, neither partner could withhold from the other the "debt of the flesh,"[61] and this payment of both fidelity and sexual gratification gave each act of sex an unselfish quality that compensated for and even overcame the lust involved.[62] In his concept of fidelity, one can again see the degree to which Augustine is holding sexual intercourse as a positive good. Essentially, the act of giving oneself freely to one's spouse redeemed the lust, which Augustine saw as the "wound" of original sin. This is strikingly different from the early Fathers, who saw hope for spirituality only in the total avoidance of sexuality. For Augustine, the benefit of fidelity overcame even the problem of men or women who had "immoderate" desires and demanded an excessive payment of the marriage debt,[63] even if they

asked for intercourse during otherwise forbidden times like menstru-
ation, during pregnancy, after menopause,[64] or during Lent.[65]

However, Augustine believed that the institution of marriage itself
cooled the fires of lust. He said marriage "... usually abates the
concupiscence of the flesh and imposes moderation on its reins. ..."[66]
Furthermore, in a psychologically perceptive observation, the Bishop
said that when husbands and wives have sex "they think of themselves as
mother and father," which makes them conduct the act with more
"dignity."[67] In many ways, then, marriage would ameliorate lust and
permit a sexual relationship that would approximate as closely as possible to prelapsarian intercourse. Such "conjugal chastity" would involve
intercourse as passionless as possible, a joining together in a spirit of
friendship rather than lust.

Once Augustine had established the nature of virtuous sex, he also
explored the characteristics of sexuality misused. Obviously, the misuse
of sex involved doing the opposite of all the things he had identified as
proper. Sex outside marriage, whether fornication or adultery, was
forbidden,[68] for that would violate the benefit of fidelity.

Even more basic than this, however, was Augustine's fear of sexual
intercourse in which lust takes over completely and overcomes reason.
This always happens to some degree in sexual activity:

> [D]oes not this extremity of pleasure result in a kind of submersion of the
> mind itself, ... since in its very operation it allows no one to think, I do not say
> of wisdom, but of anything at all?[69]

But Augustine did feel that even beyond this temporary loss of rational
thought in any sex act, it was possible for lust to reign totally, and this
was sex wrongfully used. He described this type of intercourse vividly:

> This lust assumes power not only over the whole body, and not only from the
> outside, but also internally; it disturbs the whole man, when the mental
> emotion combines and mingles with the physical craving, resulting in a
> pleasure surpassing all physical delights. So intense is the pleasure that when it
> reaches its climax there is an almost total extinction of mental alertness; the
> intellectual sentries, as it were, are overwhelmed.[70]

It was this abandonment to lust that led people into other misuses of
God's gift of sexuality. For example, lust could drive couples into using
birth control methods,[71] like placing willow seeds in wine.[72]

Lust could also stir people to other "unnatural" sexual acts in
addition to birth control. Augustine warned that there are some kinds of
intercourse which are "contrary to nature," "damnable" and "abominable." His only clarification of this type of intercourse was "when the

husband wishes to use the member of his wife which has not been given for this purpose. ...."[73] Augustine here was probably referring to any kind of non-genital intercourse, but his general statement regarding unnatural kinds of intercourse led to much speculation from subsequent medieval writers as to exactly which sexual positions and variations might be acceptable or prohibited.[74]

Augustine's views on what constituted good and bad sex – indeed, even the fact that he would consider the question – derives from his revolutionary view of original sin. This view rescued sexuality from the completely negative dualistic perspective of the early Fathers. Along with this changed perception of sex came a differing view of women. Since Augustine's model of sexuality was much more complicated than the dualistic one, so was his view of women. He did not simply relegate them to the carnal world as temptresses, leaving men as the more spiritual beings. In fact, as we have seen, Augustine saw the manifestation of lust more clearly in men's erections than in women's bodies, but for him sexuality was natural to both sexes,[75] and he recognized that women had sexual needs which husbands should recognize.[76] Unlike the early Fathers, though, Augustine noted that continence "... has usually been pleasing to the woman, but does not please the man."[77] This observation that perhaps men's sexual needs were greater than women's was in striking contrast to the early Fathers' attribution of the primary sexual urge to women.

The early Fathers wanted to control women in part to control the sexuality that was their nature. Just because Augustine released them from the full identification with sexuality, this did not mean that he was willing to release them from the restrictions the earlier churchmen were advocating. The overriding characteristic of women for Augustine was not their sexuality, which would tempt men from spirituality, but their weakness and their consequent necessary subordination to men. Augustine was willing to alter the Christian understanding of sexuality, but not the late Roman hierarchy of power. His analysis of the weakness of women began logically with the Fall. He said the serpent first approached Eve, "... starting with the inferior of the human pair so as to arrive at the whole by stages, supposing that the man would not be so easily gullible. ...."[78] Due to woman's weaker nature, Augustine believed that the natural bond of matrimony was a "... genuine union of the one ruling and the other obeying."[79] It was by this natural state of women's submissiveness that Augustine was able to justify Old Testament examples of polygamy and to exclude any possibility of polyandry. He said that it was a "... hidden law of nature [that] things that rule love singularity ...," so that one slave cannot have many masters, but one master may have many slaves.[80] The metaphor Augustine uses here to describe women as slaves was seriously chosen. He believed that women were to be ruled by men in a natural hierarchy. To clarify this hierarchy further, Augustine described three bonds or unions that were similar: Christ and His church, husbands and wives, and the spirit and the flesh. In each case, ". . . the former cares for the latter . . ., and the latter waits on the former."[81]

Women were not only to be subject to men's control, but were to be passive in a model consistent with late Roman gender expectations. Augustine's metaphor for women's passivity was that they were "vessels."[82] As "vessels" women were the passive receptacles of men's passion, but Augustine felt that men's power brought with it a certain responsibility for the woman: "Husbands . . . pay honor to the weaker and subjected vessel. . . ."[83] But women were subjected nevertheless.

The early Fathers set men apart from women on the basis of carnality versus spirituality; Augustine set men and women apart on the basis of power. When one turns to the question of these men's various approaches to virginity and the lifestyle of virgins, it was clear that the early Fathers' views on these subjects were shaped by their views of sexuality. It remains to be explored how Augustine's change in the perception of sexuality affected his prescriptions for the women who would be living chaste lives.

Although Augustine's belief in the naturalness of sexuality might suggest that he would not have been such an advocate of virginity as were the early Fathers, this was not the case. Augustine's own conversion to Christianity was tied in his own mind to his renunciation of lust and the power it held over him. In his *Confessions* Augustine described how he had prayed to God for chastity, saying: "'Give me chastity and continence, but not yet.' For I was afraid that you would answer my prayer at once and cure me too soon of the disease of lust. . . ."[84] When he did finally receive the grace to renounce sexual relationships, he felt his conversion was completed[85] and he was subsequently baptized. Augustine's own experience of being too distracted by lust to feel himself truly prepared to follow Christ led him to tell Julian: "The evil of carnal concupiscence is so great that it is better to refrain from using it than to use it well [that is, in marriage]."[86] So Augustine did, indeed, value virginity and chastity, and accepted the older hierarchical sequence of virgin, widow then wife.[87] Yet he changed the premiss under which chastity was valued. Instead of placing the virgin in a separate spiritual state, she or he expressed an ethical choice in a world not so sharply divided between good and evil, spiritual and carnal.[88]

One of the fundamental differences between Augustine's approach to chastity and that of the early Fathers is that Augustine believed (no doubt drawing from his own experience) that it was impossible to be

continent by one's own efforts.[89] Thus in his view, all Jerome's exhortations to fast in order to conquer one's lust would be to no avail.[90] This
emphasis on the necessity for grace over one's own efforts grew out of
Augustine's position against the Pelagians, who believed that sin was not
physically inherited, so people could exert free choice.[91] For Augustine,
the main responsibility was to acquire sufficient wisdom to recognize the
gift of continence when it was received.[92] This stress on wisdom really
recalls Augustine's dichotomy of placing reason opposed to passion. In
this case, reason cannot completely control lust, but reason can work
with God's grace to do so.

Augustine's belief in the necessity for grace to overcome passion
looks back to his position on original sin in another way as well. Since
man's original sin was not sex but pride, whenever one succumbs to
pride one re-creates the original sin which introduced lust in the first
place. It is this association of pride with lust that makes it particularly
important, in the Augustinian view, for the celibate to avoid the sin of
pride. The Bishop said that it was prideful to think that one could
achieve a chaste life by one's own efforts – for example, by fasting.[93] In
fact, he said that the only use for fasting was "... that the soul may be
more humbled in prayer. ..."[94] To succumb to pride in thinking that
fasting would control lust would be to succumb to original sin, so the
only hope for a really chaste life was to be sufficiently humble to recognize the need to bow to God's will rather than exalt one's own. Augustine's tract "Holy Virginity" is really a long treatise on humility. In fact,
he noted that someone might say of his treatise that "... this is not to
write on virginity, but on humility." He agreed that this was so because
humility was really the central aspect of virginity.[95] The humility to bow
oneself to God's will and accept the gift of chastity was for Augustine
the only way to overcome the original sin of pride and its consequence,
lust. The accent on the humility of a virgin, her mental rather than her
physical state, provided the foundation for Augustine's more concrete
considerations of the ideal lifestyle for dedicated virgins.

For Augustine, unlike Jerome, a woman did not escape her carnal
nature by remaining physically pure, nor was dedicated virginity to be a
way of avoiding the responsibilities and cares of a woman's place in the
world. Jerome had listed the trials and cares of marriage and child-
bearing as good reasons for espousing virginity. Augustine disagreed
with those reasons, saying that one should not attempt to use virginity to
avoid the cares of marriage. The only legitimate reason was to think of
the afterlife, not to expect benefit in this life.[96] In fact, as we have seen,
Augustine believed that a woman could not actually choose to live a
chaste life; she had to be called to it by God's grace.

The gift of continence did not exempt a woman from all the natural demands of this world. She had not escaped the world; she had only chosen to follow one of the normal variations of life. For example, one of the main natural urges that Augustine said sex filled was the need for friendship. Virgins did not escape this need. Augustine said that in previous times people had to get married to satisfy the need for friendship, but this was no longer necessary: "But now, since the opportunity for spiritual relationship abounds ...' people could have friendship and still be continent."[97] Virgins still needed companionship; as women they still remained bound to subservience to men, and as members of the Church they were bound to direction from their priest. It is no wonder that Augustine was so firm in his reprimand of Ecdicia, the chaste matron with whom this book began. She was using her chastity to avoid her traditional female responsibilities. For Augustine, she could be called to chastity only for benefit in the next life, not for convenience or freedom in this one.

Once a woman had been called to a life of chastity, Augustine had definite ideas about how she should live out her vows. The source of the Augustinian "rule" for virgins is his letter No. 211, written late in his life (about 423) to a community of consecrated virgins. As a woman joined a community of virgins, the first requirement was that she renounce all her property. Everything, even clothing and underclothing, was to be held in common.[98] Augustine stressed the importance of forgoing property and giving alms freely, because he believed that covetousness could become a substitute for sexual pleasure, as he warned in his tract on widowhood: "[W]hen carnal desire is denied gratification in sensual pleasure, it often seeks satisfaction with greater energy in the love of money. ..."[94] So by sharing their property, women might avoid substituting one pleasure for another.

The virgin's clothing must be inconspicuous in keeping with her humble bearing. Her hair must be veiled, and Augustine's admonitions on the nature of the veil suggest that some virgins saw in their veils an opportunity for some style. Augustine particularly warned that the veils might not be transparent enough for a hairnet underneath to show,[100] or – perhaps even worse – transparent enough to reveal the hair done stylishly in "little braids."[101]

Dressed thus modestly, the women were to eat their meals together and use this time educationally to listen to readings.[102] The meals should not be sumptuous, but a virgin should fast only "as far as health allows,"[103] to avoid fasting becoming a source of pride in one's capacity for renunciation. In their day-to-day lives women were to pray, read, do good works, weave and make clothing[104] – in other words, virgins leading lives dedicated to God were supposed to do all the things pious Christian wives were to do. By setting themselves apart as little as possible from normal female activities, virgins could more easily avoid the sin of pride in their own accomplishments.

The community of women would satisfy the natural need for companionship that Augustine had seen as part of the human condition. He did have some cautions regarding the enjoyment of such companionship. He wanted to make sure close friendships did not move into sexual relationships. He warned: "The love between you ... ought not to be earthly but spiritual, for the things which shameless women do even to other women ... are to be avoided. ..."[105] Avoidance of passion and advocacy of moderation were the keys to women's spiritual life. Companionship and friendship were good in the world and they were good in the convent. Extremes in expression of those things were disruptive in the world and in the convent.

Certainly Augustine's rule was not a harsh one. Compared to Jerome's strict requirements of ascetic denial of all things carnal and his warnings to women to keep a vigilant guard against an ever-threatening sexuality, Augustine's requirements for living a life of chastity were not excessive. The difference between the two derives from their differing perspectives on sexuality. Jerome felt that a woman could and must actively do things to overcome her carnal nature. That was not Augustine's position. The moderation of Augustine's rule is expressive of his belief that rules do not help: it is grace that grants continence. More important for Augustine than any actions, then, was the necessity to bow before God's gift of chastity in an obedience that would demonstrate one's renunciation of the original sin of disobedience that had led to a sexual Fall. The virgin was to obey the superior and "... even more readily should you obey the priest who has charge of you all."[106] This stress on obedience led Augustine to say: "Greater, indeed, is the good of obedience than the good of continence"; therefore a disobedient virgin was worse than an obedient wife.[107] The early Fathers, with their careful separation of the carnal from the spiritual, would never have said that. For Augustine, however, the obedient virgin was a humble one, and thus avoided the pride that had led to Adam's initial disobedience. Only in the context of achieving humility did Augustine suggest that virgins be modestly silent: "... humility is easily preserved in listening, whereas it is hard to do it in teaching. ..."[108] This is tellingly different from the early Fathers' admonition that virgins be silent to live the metaphor of closed asexuality. For Augustine humility was central to virginity, just as pride was central to his idea of sin.

Augustine had redeemed sexual intercourse by making the original sin pride, with lust as its consequence. This meant that women living a chaste life were no longer set apart as special spiritual beings, as they had been by the early Fathers. Augustine may have freed women from being the sole source of troubling sexuality, but he did not free virgins from strict adherence to rules. His virgins were women, humble and obedient vessels of God's grace, but bound to their roles as women as surely as their married sisters. The virgin life was not to be an emancipating one; the yoke of virginity was as demanding as the bonds of matrimony.

PART II

The Virgins

Introduction

Although the early Fathers and Augustine had differing views of sexuality, their conclusions on how virgins should live were similar. Whether a woman remained silent to live out the metaphor of closed asexuality or as an expression of humility, she was silent nevertheless. Whether she was obedient to fulfill her expected role as a woman or to express an abnegation of will, she was compliant nevertheless. The Augustinian revolution in perceptions of sexuality represented only a minor change in rules for chaste women.

All the Fathers developed their theoretical positions in response to a historical reality in which there had always been some women who ignored patristic exhortations. In fact, the patristic rhetoric was so prolific precisely because some virgins were behaving in ways inconsistent with the Fathers' understanding of asexual womanhood. Tertullian's repeated command that virgins veil themselves was a response to the fact that virgins dedicated to God were not wearing veils. Jerome's preoccupation with virgins traveling and mingling with the worldly derived from the fact that many were doing so. Finally, Augustine's caution that virgins not fall into the sin of pride was directed at those who were proud of their status and expressed this pride by unfeminine independence. These women were living an ideal of virginity different from that of the Western Fathers, and indeed older than the patristic writings.

This alternative ideal survived in the legends that told of ascetic women's lives and is more difficult to study than the patristic one, because the tenets were neither clearly articulated nor preserved in polemic tracts. We would not have access to this alternative thought, except through negative patristic references (like Augustine's reprimand of Ecdicia), had not a number of people continued to respect the Eastern ascetic tradition represented by the lives of independent virgins. This admiration is seen in the narratives of saints' lives that were copied and recopied, preserved and read in monasteries by men and women who lived primarily in the patristic, hierarchic model of spirituality. To explore the ascetic tradition of spiritual chastity, we must turn to the narratives of women who were perceived to be holy even if they did not necessarily meet patristic standards for holy virginity. These narratives contain the argument for this alternative view expressed in historical action rather than in the polemics of patristic theory. I will accept and highlight that contrast by presenting the second half of this book in more of a narrative fashion than the first.

The stories presented here represent a range of historical accuracy. Some of the Lives, like those of Egeria, Melania, and perhaps Pelagia, are probably fairly accurate, describing actions of real women in their search for spirituality. The Life of Helia, on the other hand, is probably a purely fictional account composed to make a point about virginity. Between these two extremes lie degrees of historical precision. The Life of Constantina is a fictional life attributed to a historical person, while the Life of Mary of Egypt is a highly miraculous account which draws from several previous stories. There were certainly women ascetics living in the desert like Mary, but the probability of a "historic" Mary of Egypt is very slim. The last Life, Castissima's, may come closest to the example of Mary of Egypt, a fictional life that was a prototype of the lives of some real ascetic women. The issue of historical importance becomes even more complicated, because a saint who probably did not exist might be more influential than one who did, if the former's legend was more widely circulated. Thus Mary of Egypt, whose Life was widely copied was more consequential than Egeria, whose writings did not circulate as widely.

What is more significant than the historical reality of these women, therefore, is the fact that their legends existed, were read, were popular, and provided models for the faithful to emulate. In addition, there were various degrees of belief; many of the faithful accepted even the most incredible portions of the tales, while others took incidents, like a lion digging Mary's grave, to be metaphoric expressions of the woman's sanctity. In either case, the Lives portrayed a lesson for the medieval audience, and within this message lies a truth that transcends the question of whether each woman actually lived. That truth is the articulation of a perspective on sanctity that revealed the ascetic view of independent virginity. This is the reality I want to extrapolate from these Lives. I shall treat the narratives as the medieval audience would have, dealing only peripherally with the secondary question of whether or not the individual actually lived. The legends did live, and they reveal a view of sexuality and womanhood that provided an alternative to the patristic one.

I have arranged the seven Lives in the Spanish manuscript in an order that will show various ways in which virginity was seen in the ascetic tradition as a route to emancipation for women. Chapter 4 demonstrates how two women in the fourth and fifth centuries used ascetic Christianity to renounce the social expectations that bound them. Chapter 5 looks at women going beyond renouncing expected actions, and challenging patristic thought. Then, in "Freedom of Movement," women take the ideas implicit in "Freedom of Thought" and put them into action by traveling in violation of patristic prohibition. Finally, two women transcend their gender altogether by dressing and living as men in the ascetic world. This is the final logical consequence of women escalating their freedom from patristic definitions of them, their sexuality and their lives as virgins. In fact, it is by claiming freedom that all these women became "virgins" in the old Roman use of the word, which referred to a woman who was independent of a man regardless of whether she was a "virgo intacta" or not. It is in this sense that I refer to all these women as "virgins," even though some had been married and others were ex-prostitutes; they were virgins by virtue of the liberty they claimed with their chastity. Each of the Lives could fit into several of my fairly artificially separate categories. However, focusing on different aspects of the independence these women claimed provides a key to understanding this alternative view of sexuality and spiritual womanhood, which will be described in the last chapter.

4

Freedom from Social Expectations
Constantina and Mary of Egypt

> But now we are discharged from the law, dead to that
> which held us captive. ... (Romans 7:l6)

While the Church Fathers were articulating what it meant to be a Christian in the midst of Roman society, many women, too, were redefining
their roles. As Christ had come to set aside old Judaic Law, it seemed
that His coming had set aside many of the social expectations that bound
people. In a sensitive analysis of the ideas of freedom implicit in the
beginnings of the Bible in Genesis, Elaine Pagels writes that Christianity
"... challenged converts to break all that bound them to their families, to
their cities, to the nation – all, in short, that conscientious people ... held
most sacred."[1] The Escorial manuscript contains the Lives of two
women whose narratives particularly demonstrate the degree to which
conversion to Christianity – or, more precisely, conversion to an ascetic
Christianity involving the renunciation of sexuality – freed women from
the social expectations attendant upon their positions in Roman society.
These women were Constantina, the daughter of the Emperor, and Mary
of Egypt, a prostitute. Both of those positions in Roman society required
adherence to strict behavior expectations.

Constantina

Constantina was the daughter of Constantine the Great, and as the
daughter of an emperor much was expected of her. Judith Hallett, in
Fathers and Daughters in Roman Society, convincingly demonstrates the
importance of the father–daughter relationship among the elites in
Roman society. She writes that there was a "valuation of elite Roman
daughters, [a] ... cultural centrality of the daughter role, and [an]

emphasis on kin ties through daughters. . . ."[2] Hallett goes on to describe some of the expectations that bound these daughters of the elite. She sees the "social dimension of a daughter's role" to be one of deference and personal allegiance. Daughters were also to be sexually above reproach and to be dependent on fathers (even over husbands) for protection and support. Furthermore, in her detailed analysis of Roman daughters, Hallett finds that by and large these expectations were met.[3] If all elite Roman girls were expected to act as responsible daughters, how much more important would be the role of the daughter of the Roman Emperor, who was father to his Empire as well as to his daughter? Thus, in many ways, Constantina was bound by expectations even higher than other Roman women who chose to change their lives by converting to Christianity, and her example of rebellion against such expectations would be an influential one.

The Life of Constantina in the Escorial manuscript is a long narrative in three books (or, more accurately, chapters). The first begins with a description of Constantina, daughter of Constantine. The young girl was afflicted with leprosy. This retiring, ill daughter visited the shrine of St Agnes in Rome and the Saint appeared to her, saying: "Constantina, be constant, believe in Jesus Christ the son of God who grants health."[4] Constantina was cured at the tomb and decided to be "constant" and dedicate her virginity to Christ in imitation of the virgin martyr Agnes, whose intercession had effected her cure. She then had her father build a church dedicated to the martyr saint who saved her body and her soul.

Later, a successful Roman general, the widower Gallicanus, returned from the East in triumph and asked Constantine for his daughter's hand in marriage. Gallicanus was a great general who had conquered many of Rome's enemies. Constantine considered him worthy to be a son, and therefore looked favorably upon the General's request for Constantina's hand. As Hallett notes, the importance of the father–daughter relationship created a similarly strong tie between fathers and sons-in-law, even at the expense of the father–son relationship.[5] Thus the significance of the proposed bond between the Emperor's daughter and the Emperor's best general would not have been lost on the Roman audience. By asking for Constantina's hand, Gallicanus was in effect making a bid for the purple, and by accepting him as a son-in-law, Constantine would have foreclosed the possibility of a powerful military man becoming a rival. Instead, he was made a member of the family. The manuscript specifically says that Constantine recognized how meritorious Gallicanus would be as a son.[6] Therefore he approved the alliance, announced the engagement, and prepared to send Gallicanus back to the Front as an even more eager supporter of an Empire he might well inherit.

Constantina had already pledged her virginity to Christ, and she vigorously expressed that position to her father. This expression of willfulness went against Roman social expectations calling for obedient, compliant daughters. The Life goes even further, however, by portraying the Emperor seeking his daughter's advice on how to resolve the dispute. Constantina devised a plan to dissuade her suitor. First, she sent her two faithful Christian servants, John and Paul, to go with Gallicanus to look for an opportunity to convert the pagan General to Christianity, and to a respect for chastity. Secondly – and more importantly – Constantina asked that Gallicanus's two young daughters, Attica and Artemia, should come to live with her. Gallicanus was pleased that Constantina seemed so ready to assume her role as stepmother, but in fact the virgin planned to attempt to convert the daughters to a Christian life of chastity, and through them win over the father. By approaching the father through the daughters the author shows an awareness of the importance of the father–daughter bond, yet it is reversed by the hope that the daughters might guide the father, rather than the other way around. This directly paralleled the reversal of power in the relationship between Constantina and her father.

The young virgins arrived in Constantina's household and Constantina began their instruction with a prayer to St Agnes, who had been instrumental in her own conversion. She asked that the daughters be made receptive to her lessons, and that through them she might be freed from Gallicanus's "diabolical passion."[7] In her prayers, Constantina makes clear her reliance on the importance of the father–daughter relationship.

The longest portion of the Life concerns the education of Attica and Artemia in their progress toward the spiritual life. They read, study, and correspond with their Aunt Octavia. Their Aunt urges them to go to church, hear hymns and lessons, and follow the Old Testament model of holy matrimony. The aunt makes the sort of argument in favor of marriage that was marshalled repeatedly by parents to Christian children – a socially conservative Christian position, taken by the Church Fathers, which argued that Christianity was not incompatible with the social expectations that governed women's lives. However, the heroines of these saints' lives were not content with a Christianity that conserved the social order. Their faith was one that freed them from the past. Constantina was not content with Attica and Artemia becoming Christian matrons, for that would suggest that she should fulfill her role as Emperor's daughter by marrying her father's valued general. And she did not intend to do that.

Book I of the Life continues with a series of arguments designed to win Artemia and Attica not only to Christianity, but to the ascetic

Christianity that said virginity was the preferred way of life even if it violated all social expectations. These discussions took place in Constantina's palace, where she was surrounded by 120 virgins who lived with her in a community. The arguments took the form of opinions on what constituted the "highest good" and the "ultimate evil" for humankind. Opinions by various people were read which argued that such things as just laws, peace and truth were the highest good, and injustice, war, and ignorance were the worst evils. Constantina turned each argument to prove that the highest good was virginity and the ultimate evil was concupiscence. For example, against the premiss that war and peace represented the primary poles of human existence Constantina argued that passion is the war that disturbs humanity, and peace means a victory over passion.[8] Constantina's association of peace with virginity is a telling one. As an emperor's daughter she was supposed to be concerned with imperial peace, a peace in the public sphere. The main reason for marriages of imperial daughters was to aid in maintaining peace, and Constantine's acceptance of the General, Gallicanus, for his daughter was to enhance the security of the realm. By defining the most important peace as chastity, Constantina placed peace in the private sphere, ignoring the public one as irrelevant. She not only flouted the social expectations that were supposed to bind her, she inverted them.

While Constantina's praises of virginity ranged over many issues, one particularly confronted the question of social expectations for women. Constantina says that virgins in their souls and bodies have eminence or distinction: "In truth, virgins have so much rank in their soul that they may withstand imperial order."[9] Here she is specifically claiming her right to reject her imperial father's order to marry Gallicanus should he come back to claim his bride. Yet, more generally, Constantina's argument gave women who chose to stay virgin the right to violate all sorts of social expectations, and as we shall see, they frequently did so. An attempt to restructure the social hierarchy can also be seen in the title by which Constantina is addressed throughout the Life. She is referred to as "Augusta," her right as daughter of an emperor. However, the Life says that this title is warranted by the high status of a virgin – any virgin.[10] The rank of virginity outranked all others in earthly hierarchies.

After twenty-one disputations of opinions on the "*summum bonum*," all of which were long on rhetoric and short on logic, Gallicanus's young daughters were convinced and converted to a life of Christian chastity. Book I of the Life ends with Gallicanus's return in triumph from the foreign wars.

The second book of the Life of Constantina is preserved elsewhere as the Passion of St Gallicanus.[11] It does, however, follow logically from the narrative of Book I. The book begins with Gallicanus's triumphant return to his Emperor and to the Senate of the Roman people. Constantine noted a strange fact about Gallicanus's return and asked the General about it: "Gallicanus, when you left, you worshipped at the temple, but upon your return you worshipped at the church of the Apostles. What caused the change?"[12] Gallicanus told of a terrible battle in which the Roman legions were being defeated. Even some of the Roman tribunes began to surrender. John and Paul, Constantina's servants, seized the opportunity to speak for Christianity and perhaps convert Gallicanus in his hour of need, thus possibly fulfilling their mistress's purpose. They urged Gallicanus to take a vow to God. As soon as the General had done so, a young man of immense stature appeared, carrying a cross on his shoulders. With him appeared a host of soldiers who led the legions to a victory. The enemy king, Braban, surrendered and the victory went to Rome and to the now Christian Gallicanus. After the battle, Gallicanus told the cowardly tribunes that he would restore them to their positions if they would convert to Christianity.

This generosity on the part of Gallicanus again comments on a reversal of social expectations brought about by conversion to Christianity. The tribunes had betrayed their Empire and their duty by their cowardice. They should have expected a public punishment for that betrayal. Yet Gallicanus was willing to forgive treasonous behavior for the higher good of gaining Christian converts. This is a parallel example to Constantina's consideration of the private peace of chaste Christianity as superior to the public peace of military victory. Constantina, through the efforts of her servants, had converted Gallicanus to a Christianity that caused him to violate the social responsibilities that had previously bound him.

The Life continues with the Emperor applauding Gallicanus's wisdom in dealing with the tribunes, thus throwing the weight of imperial approval behind this striking departure from expected behavior. Constantine then told Gallicanus of the conversions of Attica and Artemia and of their decision to join Constantina in a life of chastity. The newly converted Gallicanus was pleased, and the two men entered the palace to greet the pious women, Constantina, Artemia, Attica and Constantine's mother, Helena. Three generations of Christian women confronted and congratulated the men, who had been led to their faith by the strength of the women's convictions. Constantina's plan for Gallicanus had been fulfilled. Through the efforts of her servants and the examples of Gallicanus's daughters, the General was pleased to free Constantina from her father's promise. The security of Rome was to be assured not by the marriage of the Emperor's daughter to a strong general, but through a Christian general who received divine military help as a consequence of a virgin daughter's intercession. This was the moral of this part of the story.

Book II continues to follow Gallicanus's life beyond his direct connection with Constantina, yet by including it in the Life of Constantina the hagiographer seems to credit Gallicanus's accomplishments to Constantina. Her influence reached beyond events within her direct control. Gallicanus gave away his money (after endowing his daughters with an adequate income) and led a holy life helping the poor and the sick. His peaceful existence continued until the reign of Julian the Apostate, who began to persecute Christians again. Gallicanus was given the choice either to sacrifice to the old gods or go into exile. He chose the latter and went to Alexandria, where he was eventually martyred for his beliefs.

The third and final book in the Life of Constantina is elsewhere preserved as the Passion of John and Paul.[13] This book begins with the deaths of Constantine and his daughter and the beginning of the reign of Julian the Apostate. Yet the connection to Constantina remains evident. The hagiographer traces the impact of Constantina's fortune, which was left to her faithful servants, John and Paul. Her influence reached beyond the grave to help her servants provide for the poor and the sick with her money.

These Christian good works offended the new, impious Emperor, but John and Paul refused to abandon their Christianity to serve Julian. Julian gave them ten days to change their minds, a time they used to prepare themselves for martyrdom. Ten days later Julian sent his soldier, Terentianus, to compel John and Paul to worship an idol. The two, of course, refused, were martyred and secretly buried in their house so that no trace of them would be found for the impious to desecrate. Shortly afterward, Terentianus's son was possessed by a devil in punishment for his father's hand in the martyrdom. Terentianus then converted to Christianity and recorded this account of the martyrs' passion. Thus ends the Life of Constantina – or, more precisely, the legend of Constantina.

The striking degree to which this legend exemplifies a violation of social expectations on the part of a Christian virgin can be most clearly demonstrated by contrasting it with the life of the real Constantina, daughter of Constantine. In reality, the Emperor had arranged for his daughter to marry his general Hannibalianus, thus raising the General's hopes that he might someday rise to the purple. Constantine encouraged these hopes, no doubt as much to control a possible rival as to seek a worthy successor, since he had four sons of his own. Unlike the legendary Constantina, the real one married the General and the status of son-in-law brought Hannibalianus a good deal of advantage. He was given the title King of Kings and sent to rule in Pontus (between Armenia and the Black Sea) with Constantina as his queen. After Constantine's death, his son Constantius II had Hannibalianus killed, and arranged another politically expedient marriage for his sister Constantina. She was given to her cousin Gallus in marriage, again for the purpose of political alignment. Marriage to Constantina served as a means for upward mobility for Gallus for a while. He was made Caesar in 351, but fell in the political struggles that marked the years after Constantine's death. He was murdered in 353. Constantina died a year later. This brief sketch demonstrates that Constantina fulfilled the main expectation of an emperor's daughter. She was a political vehicle through which alliances were made and unmade.

Of the real Constantina's personality we know little, but if Ammianus Marcellinus is to be believed, the historical Constantina bears little resemblance to the peaceful virgin of legend. Ammianus describes her as "a Megaera in mortal guise, ... being as insatiable as he [Gallus] in her thirst for human blood." He continues to describe how she worked closely with her husband in the conspiracies that led to his murder.[14] Even these actions, however, place the historical Constantina well within the expected behavior of a daughter of Constantine in an age when the siblings were vying for power.

The legendary Constantina was in many ways a mirror image of the historical one. In the legend, the virgin refused a politically expedient marriage; in reality, the daughter accepted two such marriages. In the legend, the virgin renounced her public role as emperor's daughter to pursue private interests; in reality, the daughter threw herself into the political maelstrom that was her birthright. The legend presented an idealized version of a perfect Christian daughter who used her commitment to virginity to overturn her earthly responsibilities. This is in perfect contrast to the real daughter who conformed to her expected role and accepted the responsibilities of high position.

The striking contrast between the legend and the reality raises issues about the origin of the legend itself. Some people have posited the existence of two daughters of Constantine named Constantina and Constantia (a variant spelling that appears in the sources to refer to Constantina).[15] This solution is improbable. The historical sources refer to only one daughter with a name like this, and it is unlikely that a child of so famous an emperor would have disappeared from all historical references and be mentioned only in a saint's life. While the history of the legend of Constantina deserves more detailed study, I would like to suggest a hypothesis for its development.

Contributing to the persistence of the legend is the visible tomb of

Santa Constanza in Rome, built in the fourth century by Constantine near the Basilica of St Agnes, also built by the Emperor. This church became associated with Constantina, the Emperor's daughter, but it was most probably originally built for Constantine's half sister, Constantia.[16] Constantia was a pious Christian as well as a loyal sister to the Emperor. Like Constantine's daughter, Constantia made a politically useful marriage to Licinius, who was murdered in 324 by Constantine's order. Constantia remained a pious Christian widow after her husband's death. Constantine built the tomb of Santa Costanza shortly after the death of Licinius, when both he and Constantia were in Rome. It makes most sense that this was built to appease his pious sister, not to please his less-than-pious daughter. Yet the tomb came to be associated with Constantina, not Constantia, thus yielding a concrete example of piety to feed a legend of a Christian daughter of Constantine.

The proximity of the tomb to the burial place of St Agnes (where Constantine had a basilica built sometime before 349) contributed to popular identification of Constantina as a pious virgin like Agnes. As the legend evolved, the association between the two was more fully developed until it became as it appears in the narrative. Further association occurred between Constantina and Agnes because both Constantina and her younger sister Helena were buried in Agnes's tomb. Ammianus says that the body of Julian's wife, Helena, was sent to Rome to be buried "in his villa near the city on the via Nomentana where her sister Constantina, formerly the wife of Gallus, was buried."[17] Their bodies could have been buried in the tomb at that time, or later. In any case, the piety that led to the building of the tomb was probably Constantia's, but the reputation for piety devolved to Constantina.

The first part of the written legend was probably the Passion of John and Paul, found in Book III of the manuscript. The historical Constantina could well have left money in her will for her faithful servants (though not for any Christian motive) and John and Paul seemed to have moved to Rome and done good works with the funds. They were martyred in 362 and indeed buried in their house in Rome. The Acts of John and Paul were probably composed shortly thereafter by Terentianus. The association of the Christian martyrs with Constantina's money fueled the growth of the legend of the virgin daughter of the Emperor. After Julian the Apostate died in 363, the bodies of John and Paul were exhumed and buried properly. Their house was then converted into an oratorium. In 410, Pammachius (Jerome's correspondent) built a church over the tomb of the saints. This early church has been excavated, and reveals paintings showing the martyrdom as well as Constantina with her two servants.[18]

The associations that came to form the legend must have been made

by the sixth century, when the other two books of the Life of Constantina seem to have been composed and added to the Passion of John and
Paul.[19] The result is a portrayal of an emperor's daughter that would
have been ideal in the ascetic Christian tradition. The legendary
Constantina was the precise opposite of the real daughter, and this
reveals the degree to which Christians assumed that their religion
permitted them to overturn social expectations. The attachment of the
legend to visible monuments – the tomb of Constanza, the basilicas of
Agnes and John and Paul – contributed to the long-standing nature of
the legend.

The fame of Constantina was not limited to the East. In addition to
the Spanish manuscript that preserved the Life, a version of at least part
of the *Vita* must have reached Anglo-Saxon England at least by the
seventh century, because it was used by the famous Anglo-Saxon writer
Aldhelm. In the late seventh century, Aldhelm wrote a prose tract praising virginity for Abbess Hildelith and her nuns at Barking. He included
Constantina in his list of virgins whom he praised. Some years later,
Aldhelm wrote a verse version of the prose tract, the *Carmina de
Virginitate,* in which he expanded on some of the narratives included in
the prose work. Among those he amplified was the Life of Constantina,
and this expansion suggests that at least a portion of the *Vita* was
accessible to him.[20] He did not include the material from Book III of the
Life (the Acts of John and Paul) although he does have the material
from the other two books.[21] Aldhelm's *Carmina* was widely read and
studied in England and on the Continent until the twelfth century,[22] so
the legend of Constantina spread widely.

The fact that Constantina's reputation was built not on the actions of
the real emperor's daughter but on the piety of her aunt and her servants
does not detract from the lesson that Christ had come to establish a new
law for Christian behavior. As with so many of these saints' lives, the
legend was more important than the real individual.

Mary of Egypt

The story of Mary of Egypt follows a popular hagiographic pattern, that
of the reformed prostitute. This theme began with the Mary Magdalene
legend and continued in a long and popular tradition. Stories of
redeemed prostitutes have as their basic moral the redemptive quality of
Christianity. Through Christ, even so base a sinner as a prostitute could
become a saint. This lesson provided a metaphoric moral for all sinners
who wanted to change their lives.

The model of a reformed prostitute violates Roman social expectations as fully as an emperor's daughter who declined her role. Prostitutes were acknowledged, accepted and regulated during the Roman Empire. However, as Leah Otis observed, "A woman who had once registered as a prostitute retained that stigma for the rest of her life, even if she ceased all professional activity."[23] There was no possibility of a conversion and penance to redeem a fallen woman. An upper-class man could not marry a prostitute,[24] and the stigma extended even to the next generation, for an upper-class Roman would "suffer the brand of infamy . . ." if he were to attempt to legitimize his daughters by prostitutes.[25] It was within this context that people heard the stories of prostitutes who, by their conversion to the Christian life, not only were forgiven their previous life, but were able to transcend it. Indeed, they were "discharged from the law. . . ."[26]

The Life of Mary of Egypt was a very popular legend of this genre throughout the Middle Ages; it was translated into many languages and included in the popular *Golden Legend*, which was widely read for centuries. The Life was attributed to Sophronius, Patriarch of Jerusalem, who probably wrote it in about AD 600 after hearing the story as it had been preserved by oral tradition since Mary's death in about AD 421. By the time the Life was recorded, however, it had been considerably embellished by incidents taken from other sources – for example, some elements were taken from Jerome's *Life of Paul the Hermit*. The narrative is preserved in various forms: both Latin and vernacular versions, as well as prose and verse.[27] In all versions, there are two elements that make up the story. One is the moral embodied in the penitent prostitute, the other is the praise of the ascetic life over the coenobitic, exemplified by the monk Zosimas who found Mary in the desert. All the versions emphasize one element or the other,[28] but it is important to note that the two elements do not represent a strict dichotomy. The ascetic lesson that Zosimas learned is in the same ascetic tradition that freed Mary from the constraints of her past. The version in the Escorial manuscript emphasizes the story of the penitent, Mary. This is not surprising, since it is a manuscript that presents the strength of ascetic women.

The narrative in the Escorial manuscript introduces the Life as having been translated from Greek to Latin, and it begins with the monk Zosimas. Zosimas had lived in a coenobitic community since his childhood: he had been a good and pious monk for fifty-three years. After all this time, he was still not content with his progress toward God, and wondered how he could learn even more. He was divinely instructed to go to another monastery near the Jordan, where he might gain more insights. The new monastery adhered to even more severe rules than the one from which Zosimas had come. Among the increased austerities was the requirement that all the monks leave the monastery to spend Lent in

the desert in solitude and fasting. By this requirement, the monastery
and the hagiographer were elevating the ascetic life of solitude over the
communal coenobitic one as the path to the highest sanctity. While the
Life was directing Zosimas outward, the lesson would have held true for
women as well, because it was through ascetic Christianity, not through
the more controlled path of coenobitism, that women would take their
freedom.

Zosimas crossed the Jordan and entered the desert. After he had
wandered for twenty days, he was resting and praying at noon when he
lifted his eyes to the East. There he saw what at first he thought was a
ghost. It was a naked figure, skin blackened by the sun, clothed only in
long hair like white wool. The figure began to flee deeper into the
desert, and Zosimas pursued it. Finally he caught up with the apparition,
which then addressed him by name, saying: "Father Zosimas, why do
you chase me? Forgive me for not turning toward you, for I am a
woman nude. Lend me your cloak so I may turn toward you and accept
your prayers."[29] Zosimas was astounded that she knew his name, and he
stripped off his garment and gave it to her.

The Roman world would have recognized in the exchange of clothing
a striking violation of the rules that governed prostitutes, and therefore
governed Mary. Prostitutes were supposed to wear specific toga-like
garments to distinguish them from matrons.[30] Mary's nudity stood out in
direct contrast to the expectation. In fact, it was a renunciation of the
rules that had defined her previous existence. Her long white hair was an
even further departure from the norm. Prostitutes were to wear their
hair unveiled (unlike their matronly counterparts), and many dyed it
bright colors to call attention to the fact that it was free-flowing.[31]
Mary's defiant display of her bright white hair was a curious parody of
the prostitute's life. Her hair was bright and noticeable, but since she was
clothed in the virtue of the penitent she was even exempt from the social
expectation that matrons should bind their hair modestly. Mary's
conversion did not make her a chaste Roman matron. It made her a
saint, exempt from all Rome's social standards.

Mary and Zosimas argued over who should give the first blessing,
each pleading unworthiness in the face of the other's sanctity. After
persisting in modest self-denial for a long time, the two summed up their
arguments. Mary said: "Father Zosimas, to you the honor goes to
bestow a blessing. You who have the sacred priestly office, and for many
years have assisted at the holy altar full of holy prayers." Greatly terri-
fied and astounded, Zosimas responded: "Certainly I see, O Mother,
that you are full of the holy spirit, knowing my name and priestly office
when you've never seen me. You are proven great by your works. I join
with you through God in first accepting a benediction from you."[32]

Zosimas won the argument, persuading Mary to bless him first. The hagiographer notes that by this, Mary, the ascetic and the woman, was superior spiritually to the old, pious monk. After the exchange of benedictions, they entered into conversation.

Zosimas asked how Mary came to be in the desert, and she told her story: "Father, my country was Egypt. When I was twelve years old, I abandoned my parents and went to live in Alexandria. For seventeen years I sold my body, not to accumulate riches, but just to live a luxurious life. I abandoned myself to drinking, sleeplessness and lived a defiled life with laughter, ardor and friends."[33] The legal minimum age for marriage in the Empire (even as late as AD 530) was twelve.[34] It may have been that Mary was choosing to reject marriage and establish her independence by marketing her sexuality, just as later she would be freed from social constraints by rejecting it.

When Mary was about twenty-eight years old, she saw a group of pilgrims from Libya preparing to cross the sea. She learned that they were going to Jerusalem to celebrate the "redemption and ascension of Christ".[35] Mary was interested in the procession and wanted to join the pilgrims. She was told she could join them if she paid the passage fee, as everyone else did. She did not have enough money for the passage, having spent all her earnings in luxurious living, but she offered to earn it, saying: "You may use my body for the passage fee."[36]

The voyage was hard, but the pilgrims arrived in Jerusalem and joined the procession of the Cross that preceded the festival. At dawn on the morning of the feast day everyone hurried to the church. Mary tried to join the celebrants, but her past life caught up with her at the door of the church. A mysterious force repeatedly prevented her from entering. Her sins kept her from joining the community of the faithful. She retreated from the doorway and sat and wept, miserable at her sinfulness. Looking up, she saw an image of the Virgin Mary and prayed to her namesake for forgiveness. She renounced her previous life and was able to enter the church and worship the true Cross.

Upon leaving the church, she heard a voice saying: "If you cross the Jordan, you will find rest."[37] She felt herself divinely guided to her place of penance. A pious man gave her three coins with which she bought three loaves of bread to take with her to the desert. She crossed the Jordan with many tears of penitence and had lived in the desert ever since, seeing no one.

Zosimas asked how long she had been a hermit, and about her labors in the desert. She responded that she had been in the desert for forty years,[38] and had subsisted for that time on the loaves of bread she had brought with her. She said it was the first seventeen years that had troubled her the most. During that time she was plagued with recollections of the carnal delights she had left behind. She overcame her sordid thoughts with many tears and, armed with prayer, she vanquished her burning passions. The sweetness of overcoming these temptations more than compensated for her lack of food and clothing. She was clothed in the word of God.

Zosimas asked her if she read the Psalms or other Scriptures and she responded that she did not read, but just existed in the presence of the word of God. Zosimas was awed by the "miracles without number"[39] that surrounded Mary's life, and he fell to the ground praising God's works. At this point, the coenobitic monk learned that the miracles of the ascetic life were powerful indeed.

Before the monk left, Mary asked him to return to the Jordan on Holy Thursday of the following year to bring her holy communion. She told him to stay in his monastery during the year, but to tell no one about her until after her death. Zosimas followed her instructions and the following year he left his monastery, bringing with him the sacred Body and Blood. He went timidly, afraid he would be unworthy of seeing her. At the Jordan he saw her waiting for him on the opposite bank. Upon the monk's arrival at the shore, Mary made the sign of the Cross and walked upon the water to greet the monk. He prostrated himself on the ground as witness to the miracle he had just seen, but then he granted her the communion she had requested. She asked that he return again at the same time the following year, then walked back across the water of the Jordan as she had come.

When Zosimas returned the following year, he found her dead. He wept for the saint, but was afraid to presume to touch her holy body. Then he saw written in the sand: "Father Zosimas, bury Mary in this place, and return her to the earth. Pray for me to the Lord at whose command I left this earth on the second day of April."[40] The old man then knew she had died after she had taken the Sacred Mystery. Zosimas tried to dig a grave to satisfy her last request, but the ground was too hard. Then a large lion approached. The monk was frightened at first, until he recalled Mary's words. So he addressed the lion: "The holy woman wants me to bury her body. But I am too old to dig and I don't have a shovel."[41] The lion dug the grave and Zosimas buried the holy woman naked as she had lived, but covered with his cloak.

Zosimas returned to the monastery and told the monks everything that had happened. All who heard cried and glorified God for such a miracle. They celebrated annually the death of the holy woman. Zosimas lived in his monastery for a long time, surviving to reach a hundred years old glorifying God. Thus ends the Life of Mary of Egypt.

The prostitute who would have been bound throughout her life by her initial choice of occupation had escaped the requirements of Roman society. She did not have to wear the clothing that marked the prostitute, and not only did she escape the stigma attached to her early sexuality, she moved to the realm of the miraculous. Not only did her conversion remove her from the constraints of social expectations, it placed her beyond the constraints of natural laws. Water became solid, lions tame.

The hagiographers of Constantina and Mary of Egypt took seriously the message of early Christianity that Christ had come to replace the old law. The women's acceptance of an ascetic Christianity that involved renunciation of their sexuality meant that they no longer had to obey the old Roman traditions. This general attitude was supported by churchmen who were creating a new ethic to replace that of Rome. However, the fact that women like Constantina and Mary of Egypt used chastity – that is, the control of their own sexuality – to take control of other aspects of their lives presented a larger example to Christian women. Perhaps chastity let women control their lives in the face not only of Rome's expectations, but of anyone else's expectations as well. This is the attitude that made churchmen develop rules for virgins' actions as well as a rationale for those rules, yet there were always women who used ascetic Christianity to violate them. The subsequent chapters look at some of those women.

5

Freedom of Thought
St Helia

> Seek not to appear over-eloquent.
> (Jerome)

A certain degree of independent thought on the part of dedicated virgins is revealed simply in the fact that some women lived out their lives in ways that did not adhere to patristic prescriptions for them. Further freedom of thought was expressed by others who preserved the narratives of these women and bound them in codices that also contained patristic writings on the subject of virginity. Given the lack of resources, however, it is obviously difficult to get a clear expression of the thought of women articulating the ascetic position. However, there is a little-known saint's life that does permit the beginnings of the exploration of a theoretical position. This is the Life of St Helia.

It is likely that Helia was a fictional character created to present a distinctive point of view concerning virginity and the position of women. According to the Life, St Helia was born in Pannonia, but there is no other evidence of her existence. She was never officially canonized; she does not appear in lists of Eastern Saints, nor even in the Spanish liturgical calendars. Even though the *Vita* claims that her birthplace was in the East, Antolín, in his analysis of the Latinity of the text, argues that it was originally written in Latin.[1] This, in conjunction with the absence of any mention of Helia in Eastern sources, suggests that the Life was first written in Spain. The attribution of Helia's birthplace to Pannonia may have two possible explanations. One is that travelers to the East returned to Spain relating the story of Helia, and it was finally written down. Another is that the Saint was given an Eastern birthplace to enhance her credibility in an age that looked to Eastern ascetics as models. Pannonia would have been a reasonable choice since that was Jerome's birthplace, and the hagiographer clearly drew from Jerome.

Upon reading this *Vita*, one is immediately struck by the hagiographer's indebtedness to Jerome. In good medieval style, the hagiographer never credited Jerome directly, but felt free to draw extensively from those of Jerome's works praising virginity that were written before 400. This familiarity with Jerome's work may provide a key to the authorship of the *Vita*. At the end of the fourth century, Jerome corresponded with a couple in Spain, Lucinius and Theodora, who were both interested in leading ascetic lives and in learning from Jerome how to do so. They were apparently very anxious to receive all Jerome's work, for in 398 Lucinius, according to Jerome, "... sent six copyists ... to copy for him all that I have ever dictated from my youth until the present time."[2] However, Lucinius was not to have much time to enjoy the Jerome corpus he received from the East. He died the following year, leaving his wife, Theodora, in possession of the works. Theodora was a literate woman who was also deeply interested in the ascetic life, and particularly in sexual renunciation. She continued to correspond with Jerome and seems to have devoted the remainder of her life to serving Christ as a widow.

It is likely that Theodora was the hagiographer who wrote the Life of St Helia. The Life draws extensively from the works that would have come to Lucinius in 399: "Against Jovinian," "Against Helvidius," Jerome's letter to Eustochium and others of Jerome's letters.[3] The Life does not draw from any of Jerome's works that date after 399. Theodora apparently used the works sent to her deceased husband to develop a polemic for dedicating one's sexuality to Christ and living as a virgin, a bride of Christ. While the extensive influence of Jerome's work visible in the Life places it within the tradition of extreme advocacy of sexual renunciation that Jerome represented, the author did not merely parrot Jerome's position. The quotations from Jerome were carefully selected to give credibility to a different view of virginity, marriage and the role of women that was being articulated by the hagiographer. By carefully considering the hagiographer's selectivity in using Jerome's work, one can see that in fact a considerable freedom of thought was expressed in this Life. Jerome's words were used in a way that gave authority to a perspective Jerome himself would probably have renounced.

The outline of the story of St Helia is fairly simple. According to the *Vita*, Helia was born of a noble family in Irracio, Pannonia. Her father (about whom we hear no more) was the Metropolitan Bishop of Epiro. Helia was a beautiful maiden and as a young girl decided to be a virgin of Christ rather than marry. She wanted "not to be subject to the curse of Eve, but rather to participate in the blessings of Mary."[4] She strove toward her goal by rigorous fasts and incessant prayer. A priest visited her, recognized her vocation and provided her with sacred books to study. She pursued her studies in secret until she was discovered by her mother, who was horrified at the direction of her daughter's enthusiasm.

Then begins a long dialogue between Helia and her mother in which they argue about whether Helia should be permitted to remain chaste or forced to marry. Finally, after two books and fourteen folio pages of disputation, Helia's mother decides that the matter cannot be handled within the domestic sphere, so she brings Helia before a judge to get permission for her to be "seized as a wife."[5] In the final book, Helia is taken before the judge. The maiden's interrogation takes place in public, "watched by the world of angels and men," and in a "terrifying" voice the judge begins his interrogation. Helia, of course, was not intimidated by the judge's challenge. She continued to defend her position, and the third book of the *Vita* consists of a dialogue between Helia and the judge. The dialogue continues rather unsatisfactorily to the end of the *Vita* with neither side giving in. During the judge's final speech, he maintained his position, saying: "No woman may be saved unless it is by bearing children. Either do what scripture says, or be judged a violator of sacred laws."[6] In Helia's final speech she maintained her defiant stand, pointing out that the "impious Cain" could hardly confer salvation upon his parents, and she would trust in the spiritual fruits that would be generated by her vow of chastity.[7] While the reader might hope for a more definitive resolution of the long dialogue in which either the judge acknowledged the error of his ways or the virgin was martyred, that does not happen in either of the surviving manuscripts of this *Vita*. Both Lives, however, are followed by a short poem entitled "In praise of the same virgin." This poem was written in the first person, beginning "I am a virgin of Christ."[8] With the addition of this poem, perhaps we are to assume that Helia won the right to have as her husband one "who presides in heaven not on earth."[9]

The story line is thin, and in some ways seems an expanded version of some scenes in the Acts of Paul and Thecla, in which Thecla argues first with her mother, then with a judge, to earn the right to remain virgin.[10] Theodora may have been inspired by these Apocryphal Acts, because they were circulating in Spain by the fourth century. This shell of a story basically provides a frame upon which to weave the arguments for a virgin life. These arguments are largely drawn from the writings of Jerome, but the hagiographer does not slavishly follow the Church Father. Some material is drawn directly from Jerome; some is based on some of Jerome's points but modified in ways that change the perspective, and some of Jerome's positions are conspicuously absent, even though they were obviously available to the hagiographer. Before one can understand the independence of thought articulated in this *Vita*, these threads of intellectual antecedents must be sorted out.

Most of the material the hagiographer draws directly from Jerome consists of arguments designed to prove that virginity is the most perfect state, and that to dedicate one's sexuality to God is the highest calling. Early in the dialogue, Helia looks to biblical precedents to justify her position on the virtues of virginity. Both Helia and Jerome find Old Testament examples of the unmarried who were noted for holiness. They point to people such as Joshua, Daniel, Elijah, Gideon and others to prove that the value of chastity was marked in the Old Testament even though marriage was considered the ideal in Old Testament times.[11] They then continue the historical argument by noting that after the birth of Christ a new epoch replaced the old, thereby introducing an era in which the ideal of marriage was replaced by the ideal of virginity. Jerome points out that "... for us virginity is consecrated by the Virgin Saviour,"[12] and "... with the difference in time and circumstance one rule applied to the former [Old Testament patriarchs] another to us."[13] Thus for Helia and Jerome, the Old Testament virgins merely foreshadowed the new age. As Helia says, "Then sterility was bad, now sterility is blessed."[14] Both continue the praise of virginity from biblical examples by pointing to New Testament figures who were noteworthy and demonstrated that indeed Christ, the Virgin Saviour, had introduced a new era. Both Helia and Jerome point to John the Baptist, Paul and John as New Testament examples of the new life. The praise for virginity based upon the New Testament seems to reach its height with Jerome's praise of John the Apostle, in which he claims that John is superior even to Peter because of his virginity: "The virgin writer expounded mysteries which the married could not, and briefly to sum up all and show how great was the privilege of John, or rather the virginity in John, the Virgin Mother was entrusted by the Virgin Lord to the Virgin disciple." And again: "Peter is an Apostle only, John is both an Apostle and an Evangelist, and a prophet."[15] Helia draws this same argument from Jerome,[16] praising in the Apostle that which she would preserve for herself.

The biblical foundation laid, Helia presents an elaborate comparison of virginity with marriage, and in this she continues to draw from Jerome's work. She says: "When she accepts a spouse, a woman is called away from the house of God; a virgin remains joined with Christ. Marriage is in Adam: virginity is in Christ. Marriage is death; virginity grants salvation. Marriage is pain; virginity is benediction. ..."[17] Jerome expresses these views in his letter to Eustochium in which he points out the advantages of a virgin life over a married one[18]; also, in his tract "Against Jovinian," he equates marriage with death and virginity with salvation, as Helia does.[19] Both Jerome and Helia sum up the dichotomy by saying: "For marriage fills the earth; but heaven is filled with virginity."[20]

Virginity's favorable comparison with marriage yields for Jerome, as well as for the other Fathers, an evaluative hierarchy of women's roles, as we have seen. Virgins are placed at the highest level, followed by widows, and finally by married women.[21] Helia shared this hierarchical view[22] and decided that in her life she would accept nothing but the highest level, that of dedicated virginity. She accepted the role of bride of Christ that Jerome assigned to holy virgins, and said: "If it is wise for a daughter to surrender to a man, why not consecrate myself to Christ, whose virtue and wisdom is from God."[23] Helia further argued that since she had dedicated herself to be Christ's bride, if she were to marry, she would be committing adultery.[24]

It is clear that what the hagiographer of the Life of St Helia took directly from Jerome were the theoretical arguments that justified, and indeed praised, the celibate life. The hagiographer also recognized that this position would not remain unchallenged even though it carried the weight of so profound a thinker as Jerome, so she also drew from Jerome its defense. The dialogue structure of the *Vita* itself represents an acknowledgement of the fact that praise of a virgin life was not universally accepted. Helia's mother represents the devil's advocate who posits arguments against the celibate life for Helia to demolish. Many of the arguments used by Helia's mother were attributed by Jerome to his critics, Jovinian and Helvidius,[25] so Helia's position is enhanced not only by her use of arguments which Jerome had refuted, but by her mother's association with people who had been shown by Jerome to be outside the doctrine of the Church as he was articulating it. So, even though Helia echoed Jerome's lament that she was being falsely accused of denigrating marriage,[26] in fact Jerome's victory over the critics of his anti-nuptial position was Helia's victory over her mother, the judge, and anyone else who might try to deny her the right to live a virginal life.

If this were all the material in the *Vita*, it would have been only a restatement of Jerome's praise of the virgin life. But the hagiographer went further. In a number of instances, she began with a statement by Jerome and then expanded it in ways that moved beyond the original text. It is in these points that the *Vita* begins to reveal an interesting perspective of its own. In the dialogue, Helia expands on some of Jerome's statements in ways that add an appreciation of women and a sensitivity to women's position. One of the most vivid examples of an elaboration of female imagery is Helia's association of virginity with fertility. As we have seen, the associations between fertility and its apparent opposite, virginity, are not new with Helia; there was a long tradition of such associations in Iberia and elsewhere. Jerome acknowledged the relationship and, for example, urged Eustochium to be, like God Himself, "fruitful in singleness."[27]

Helia, however, makes the image more concrete. Her associations present the "spiritual fruits" that would be generated by abstinence in a vivid, physical way that seems to embrace the physical nature of childbirth as Jerome never does. Helia explains the nature of her virginal condition with physical images: "God is my farmer. If in this little clod of earth of my body he wishes to plant virginity, shall I resist his labors? For no one can resist the power of the omnipotent farmer."[28] So, like the Virgin Mary, Helia was pregnant, but the children she would bear would be spiritual, and she would bear them without pain and corruption of the body.[29] Helia continues to praise enthusiastically the spiritual fruits that would accrue by her renunciation: "Behold that earth, that is, virginity, which by not being sown, will bring forth fruit a hundredfold in abundance."[30] She generously expands her praise to the whole world, not worrying whether her enthusiastic image sounds plausible: "Happy childbirth for the men, the women, the old who are made fecund; who propagate not through intercourse but through abstinence. ..."[31] In this last passage, Helia in a sense sees a life of chastity as making everyone a woman with the woman's capability of reproduction, rather than seeing the asexual life as rendering everyone male, as the early Fathers had done. Even the phrase "happy childbirth" provides a striking contrast to Jerome's perception of the whole process. Jerome described one of the worst of Christ's humiliations, to be in the womb: "... [to be in] the womb for nine months growing larger, the sickness, the delivery, the blood, the swaddling clothes. Picture to yourself the infant in the enveloping membranes."[32] When Jerome used the concrete it was to conjure up disgust, not to praise the ability to be fecund.

In fact, for all Jerome's praise of holy virgins and widows and his extensive correspondence with women, his writings reveal a revulsion at women's bodies and their sexuality. He praised celibate women because they were able to transcend their sexuality, and by so doing they could transcend their gender. The skill of Helia's hagiographer was that she could draw from Jerome, and from seeds in his thought create a work that dignified women. The fertility associations are expressed with such joy that there is no underlying rejection of women's capacity to bear children.

Helia further praises women by beginning with Jerome's identification of the three stages of womanhood – virgin, wife and widow – and developing the tripartite structure in a curious departure from Jerome by associating the three stages with the Trinity. She begins her identification of women's roles with a religious unity by referring to the passage from I John that speaks of the three things that bear witness on earth: "Spirit, water and blood, and these three are one."[33] Helia equates virginity with spirit, widowhood with water, and the married state, "which properly begets children is confirmed in the order of blood. And all these grades are one. They are not merely harmonious but properly one body, ... a unity in three."[34] Thus for Helia, the three stages of a woman's life were harmonious and a unity, but a unity of potential. These were possible choices for a woman, and each had a different worth, but a worth nevertheless. Helia, of course, followed Jerome in favoring virginity, but the trinitarian association enhanced all three and certainly dignified all women.

Helia's appreciation of the position of women is also evident during her dialogue with the judge. The judge points to scriptural law recommending marriage, saying: "it is better to marry than burn." Helia follows Jerome in indicating that laws are not always equally applicable. She argues: "It is true that scripture says it is better to marry than burn; but not for all, that is, not for sacred virgins. ..."[35] Jerome had urged Eustochium to respond to such arguments similarly by decreeing: "that is a law for married women, not for sacred virgins."[36] In Helia's dialogue, however, the hagiographer keeps the spirit of Jerome's argument for differing legal applications, but elaborates the thought to show an awareness of women's position before the law during the late Empire. Helia completes her defense by saying: "While one group submits to some laws, another group may not. How is it that some laws promulgated for women do not constrain men?"[37] She has built upon Jerome's work not only to argue for women's ability to choose celibacy, but also to comment sympathetically on their position in society. This goes well beyond Jerome's intention.

There are several other examples of the hagiographer's concern with the role of women in society, but one more should serve to demonstrate the pattern. Jerome had presented briefly an argument by Jovinian that Solomon was great even though he had many wives.[38] Jovinian had used that example merely to indicate that marriage was no hindrance. Helia's mother, who repeatedly articulated Jovinian's position, drew from the Solomon example and expanded it in a way that made a statement about the role of women in society. She attributed Solomon's greatness to women: "Before he was married, he led a private life. After he was embraced by a woman he became an effective king; he grew in wisdom and built a temple." So for Helia's mother, not only did Solomon's wives not hinder him, they helped him, and she urged her daughter to follow biblical precedent and to assume her role as "man's helper." Helia rejected the argument and the role: "If a woman was the cause of Solomon's greatness, then when he was ruined was that also caused by a woman? No, it was all God's plan."[39] Within Helia's mother's argument there was an attempt to define women's roles in terms of men's achievements. Helia's refutation seems to be a desire to establish an independent role for herself, just as other virgins in the ascetic tradition were doing. Helia intended to achieve spiritual perfection for herself, not help someone else to do so. In Jerome's use of Solomon as an example, however, there was no reflection on women's roles in society.

Beyond the question of women's role in society is the question of the role of the individual woman. In this the hagiographer departs most radically from Jerome's texts. Within the dialogue, Helia draws from Jerome on the issue of free choice. It is up to the individual woman to choose her way of life. Helia says that the "sacrifice of celibacy and virginity may not be commanded," and Jerome had said the same thing.[40] While Helia and Jerome both established a woman's right to choose her way of life, they departed rather dramatically on the way she was supposed to live once the decision had been made. As we have seen, Jerome had a great deal to say about how virgins were to live in order to preserve their chastity. In fact, the purpose of his letter to Eustochium was to establish a series of rigid guidelines that would provide a rule for women who wished to live as dedicated virgins.

Helia's hagiographer had access to this letter and used elements of it to prove the superiority of the virgin life, but she ignored its main purpose and omitted all the instructions on the way of life. This selection of materials was in spite of the fact that in that letter Jerome specifically said: "... our purpose [in writing] is not the praise of virginity but its preservation. ..."[41] However, the hagiographer drew from the letter only those things that praised virginity. In establishing a series of rules to govern a woman's dress, diet, activity and frame of mind, Jerome was describing features that were not incidental to a life of chastity, but central to it. All the rules Jerome had laid out were framed so that a woman might remain virgin in spirit as well as in body.[42] Helia's hagiographer, however, ignored Jerome's concerns by omitting all references to how a virgin should live, making it sufficient that Helia preserve her physical virginity and not worrying about whether or not she was virgin "in spirit."

In spite of the conspicuous absence of material that Jerome felt was central, it would be difficult to demonstrate a position solely from material omitted from a text, since there could be any number of reasons for not using portions of a work. However, there is evidence that the hagiographer consciously wanted to use only those arguments that would advocate virginity as a means to dignify women in general, and would not restrict the freedom that came with being unmarried. Jerome's view of the perfect virgin as expressed in his letter to Eustochium was a woman who, among other things, was silent and humble. When the hagiographer mentioned these points, she arranged for Helia's mother to articulate them.

For example, Helia's mother warns her daughter against relying on her skill in argument: "It is true that eloquence does not preclude sin . . ."[43] In much the same way, Jerome cautioned Eustochium not to "seek to appear over-eloquent."[44] Similarly, it was Helia's mother who argued that humility was necessary for salvation,[45] just as Jerome pointed out the necessity of humility for a true virgin.[46] Throughout the *Vita*, Helia's mother's function was to provide arguments for Helia to destroy. It was Helia's mother who presented the anti-chastity arguments of Jovinian and Helvidius that provided the foil for Helia to make her case by drawing on the same arguments that Jerome had used. By having Helia's mother express some of Jerome's recommendations for how a virgin was to live, the hagiographer subtly discredits those positions. The holy virgin presented by the hagiographer is outspoken, proud and independent, which is certainly not the portrait drawn by Jerome. By the subtlety of Helia's arguments, she was advocating that women – at least some women – should exert their will and obey their conscience regardless of the dictates of social convention (her mother) or society's laws (the judge). This position was contrary to the prevailing patristic view that virgins (as well as other women) would be humble, obedient and silent.

The Life of St Helia shows that a work can be indebted to patristic thought without being a carbon copy of that thought. The hagiographer of this Life used Jerome's writings as soft clay from which she shaped a work that revealed a perspective dramatically different from Jerome's. She followed Jerome exactly to develop the theoretical position that virginity was a valid – indeed, preferred – lifestyle. She built upon and modified those aspects of Jerome's thought that dealt with the position of women in society in ways that showed an awareness of the realities of this position, and dignified women and their roles. Finally, she departed most radically from Jerome when it came to the individual woman and how she was to live out her chosen role as dedicated virgin. In the use of Jerome's writings the work was enhanced by Church authority, and in the careful selection of those writings the work could express the view of the hagiographer and reveal the existence of a different perspective on womanhood and virginity from that of the Church Fathers who dominated the literature of the time. Theodora, or whoever wrote the Life, showed that she was not bound to patristic perceptions of virginity. The author revealed a freedom of thought that formed the foundation of the other liberties claimed by some ascetic women.

6

Freedom of Movement
Egeria and Melania the Younger

Go not from home nor visit the daughters of a
strange land. (Jerome[1])

A tradition of Christian travel, or travel for the sake of Christ, began
with the growth of the Church itself. The apostles left everything to
follow Christ and move about in His mission. As time passed, there
developed several ways to use travel for the sake of one's spiritual health.
Perhaps the most familiar was to go on a pilgrimage to holy places in
order to acquire some sanctity by proximity with existing holiness. A
pilgrimage could be made to any shrine containing relics of a saint, but
until the seventh century the most efficacious pilgrimage was to the Holy
Land, to the places that had been made holy by the footsteps of Christ
Himself.[2]

Another form of holy travel was for someone to move outside society
to uninhabited areas to seek God. By removing oneself from society and
becoming a stranger to human company, one could perhaps become
closer to God. In fact, such removal, even if only temporary, was one of
the requirements of a holy person in the traditional ascetic view. The
famous exemplar, St Antony, moved to the desert and established a
pattern for aspiring holy people. The *Sayings of the Desert Fathers* and
Palladius's *Lausiac History* both sustained the lesson by their many
examples of holy men and women who had moved – or, rather, removed
themselves – from society. In this category, we find the many desert
fathers and mothers who sought solitude and sanctity in Palestine or the
deserts of Egypt.

However, this sort of pilgrimage to the fringes of society was not
limited to the East. Holy people in the West also moved to the fringes of
society, whether it was to the mountains in north-west Spain, as did
sixth-century holy men, or the windswept islands in the North Sea,

83

populated by sixth-century Irish monks. However, during the early centuries of Christianity the Eastern deserts provided the best-known harsh training ground for sanctity. Of course, once the deserts had been claimed by holy people, they too became sites for pilgrimage. Certainly, as early as the fourth century, pilgrims traveled to seek out desert ascetics, and receive spiritual strength or advice from these living saints.

Yet, as we have seen, the early Western Fathers were not comfortable with women moving about so freely, even in the service of sanctity.[3] Women were told to seek holiness by staying inside their homes and not traveling at all. The principle of enclosure, which was in fact what the Fathers were advocating, suggested that for women sanctity was to be found within – both within bodies that were to remain closed sexually and within rooms that were closed to the world. According to the Fathers, aspiring holy virgins were to move away from society, but their movement was to be inward and indoors rather than to the fringes of settlement. Women were to move inside to find a sanctuary in which to keep their sanctity (and their chastity) inviolate. The principle of withdrawal was the same, but the location was different.

There were always some women who did not follow patristic suggestion in this matter. The Escorial manuscript contains accounts of two women who particularly exemplify the freedom of movement that they claimed as part of their commitment to a chaste life. Both these women, Egeria and Melania the Younger, first established a degree of sanctity by their vows of chastity. Chaste sanctity, then, gave them license to move about, and they enhanced their sanctity further by pilgrimages to the Holy Land. If along the way they enjoyed their travels, as they certainly did, then so much the better. Their chastity and sanctity had brought them a freedom and mobility that demonstrated to some women the advantage of an ascetic life over a married one.

Fortunately both these Lives are accessible in good English editions,[4] for they are quite long. Here I shall summarize the stories in a way that focuses on the nature of their pilgrimages to sanctity.

Egeria

We know very little about the pilgrim Egeria. We have no knowledge of her life, nor of how she came to be a dedicated virgin of God. Essentially, all we know about her is that she left north-west Spain and traveled through the Holy Land for three years between 381 and 384.[5] During her travels she wrote letters to her "sisters," no doubt women with whom she lived in a loose-knit community. Egeria seems to have been very fond of her spiritual sisters, for she addressed them affectionately in her letters. She called them "reverend ladies, my sisters," "loving sisters," "loving ladies," and the "light of my heart."[6] Plainly Egeria had strong ties at home; for her the call to a virgin life was not a lonely one. Fortunately for us, she had people with whom to correspond, for what appear to be two of her letters have survived. One describes her pilgrimage to holy places, the other describes the liturgical practices she saw on her way.

In her letters, Egeria said nothing about her commitment to a life of chastity, but that is not remarkable since it would have been taken for granted by her and her correspondents. Subsequent readers of her narrative (including medieval ones) assumed that she was a dedicated virgin because she had the freedom to travel, she sought out holy places in her voyages, and her correspondents were addressed as her "sisters." The first obvious piece of information available from Egeria's writings is that she believed strongly in pilgrimages. She had traveled to the Holy Land to retrace the steps of as many biblical figures as she could. She climbed Mount Sinai and stood where "the law was given, and the place where the Glory of the Lord came down on the day when the mountain was smoking."[7] She was shown "everything which the Books of Moses tell us took place in that valley beneath holy Sinai, the Mount of God."[8] By her travels, Egeria was claiming the biblical past and making it tangibly part of her own experience. She spent years doing this, and her yearnings led her to sites as spectacular as the heights of Sinai and Horeb to more modest recollections of the holy past, like Jacob's well where Rachel had drawn water.[9] Egeria was also fascinated by present holiness. She visited holy men and women at all the famous pilgrimage sites and in the deserts where they had retreated from society to live "indescribably excellent" lives.[10] She was awed by their sanctity, but curious enough about them to approach them in their cells, talk to them and receive from them "eulogiae," souvenir gifts from holy people – in this case apparently fruits or small loaves of bread.[11]

Like other pilgrims, Egeria enjoyed her travels. She wrote vividly of the wonderful things she had seen and done, and these exuberant descriptions often had nothing to do with the spiritual good that presumably was being accrued during these wanderings. She enthusiastically described the mountainous terrain and the fertile valleys, and when it was time for her to return home she stayed in order to make a detour to north-west Syria and Mesopotamia to prolong her travels.[12] Unlike many pilgrims, however, Egeria was no ascetic. As a matter of fact, she does not seem to have had much concept of asceticism before she went to the Holy Land, for she described particular holy people who were greater than regular monks, explaining to her sisters that these were called "ascetics."[13] It was not just the word that Egeria was unfamiliar with; the concept of self-punishment itself seems to have been foreign to her, since her pilgrimages lacked the self-imposed hardships that marked many others. When Egeria traveled, she rode on horses or asses. She took this form of travel for granted, mentioning it only when the paths were so steep – like climbing Mount Sinai or Nebo – that she had to dismount and "climb laboriously on foot."[14] Egeria's description of her only hardship clearly reveals the degree to which her travels were not an ascetic exercise.

There were other ways in which Egeria did not follow an ascetic model. For example, she did not value solitude for herself (although she certainly admired ascetics who could live alone). Egeria traveled in company, for she repeatedly used the pronoun "we" in her narrative. Furthermore, everywhere she went, many men joined her to show her the sights and guide her to the locations she wanted to see. Although we do not know Egeria's social background, she must have come from a fairly prestigious Hispano-Roman family,[15] for wherever she journeyed she was well received by dignitaries like the Bishop of Edessa and the Bishop of Charrae, who both accompanied her personally to pilgrimage sites.[16] When Egeria and her company were traveling through remote areas they had an escort of Roman soldiers to guard them.[17] Beyond these escorts of some prestige, it seems that at every site a variety of holy men, from clergy to monks to ascetics, joined them for a time in their visits.[18]

Traveling in such state through the Holy Land must have caused quite a stir among the local people. In fact, Egeria seems to have been quite young, if the naive enthusiasm of her narrative is any indication. It would not be surprising if there were some concern about the impropriety of a woman traveling in the company of so many men, even if they were of holy repute. Egeria seems to have indirectly addressed the possibility of gossip by assuring her correspondents that the monks never even discussed anything other than stories from Scriptures or Acts of holy men.[19] We will never know, of course, if Egeria's assurances were a bit of over-protesting or whether in fact the large retinue traveled in the most spiritual manner. However, in the Holy Land there seems to have been at least one critic of Egeria's behavior, the irascible critic of almost everything, Jerome.

Jerome arrived in the Holy Land a year after Egeria's journey, and toured many of the same places that she had visited. He does not mention Egeria directly in any of his voluminous correspondence, but that is not surprising since she had already left and he did not meet her. However, Morin argued convincingly that Jerome did refer to Egeria in his letter No. 54 to Furia, written in 394. Furia was a widow, and Jerome wrote to warn her of the dangers she should avoid. Among those dangers was the possibility of scandal. As an example of such scandal, Jerome wrote: "I have lately seen a most miserable scandal traverse the entire East. The lady's age and style, her dress and mien, the indiscriminate company she kept, her dainty table and her regal appointments bespoke her the bride of a Nero or of a Sardanapallus."[20] Jerome goes on to concede that he does not know whether there was any truth to these rumors, but he assures Furia that if rumors are false, they will quickly die down.

Morin claims that this reference to a woman causing a scandal in the East probably referred to Egeria. She was young, she did travel in some style, and she associated with many men during her pilgrimage.[21] Morin's argument was based in part on his belief that Egeria's pilgrimage took place in 394, the same year Jerome wrote to Furia. Devos's more convincing dating places Egeria in the Holy Land a decade earlier, and J.N.D. Kelly claims that the revision in the dating might well call into question Morin's identification of Egeria as the pilgrim disapproved of by Jerome.[22] Yet Morin's argument does not rest primarily on the dating. The fact that Jerome retraced Egeria's steps shortly after she had left makes it very probable that he would have heard about her travels. The fact that he waited for a time before describing the rumor to Furia does not negate the possible association. In any case, Jerome's disapproval of a pilgrim who traveled as Egeria did, whether it was she or someone else, reveals much about the discrepancy between his view of how virgins should live and the view expressed in the Escorial Lives.

Jerome's objection is consistent with everything he believed about how women – and especially virgins dedicated to God – should act. Not only did Egeria violate one of his fundamental principles – that virgins should remain enclosed at home so that they should not tempt men or be exposed to temptation – but in her travels she did not even adhere to a standard of asceticism that helped to redeem Paula, Jerome's traveling companion, and other traveling women in Jerome's eyes.

Given how little was recorded about Egeria and how little she conformed to any particular standards of holiness – except for her vows of chastity – one might ask how she found her way into a manuscript of examples of autonomous women who earned their independence by adhering to an ideal of ascetic sanctity. In fact, even Egeria's vow of chastity may well have stemmed from a desire to live independently in a company of women rather than any real call to holiness. What, then, qualified her to be included in the Escorial manuscript?

Egeria's own narrative of her travels was not included in the manuscript. However, this narrative was read in the early seventh century by Valerius of Bierzo, a Spanish holy man and abbot who adhered to and advocated an ascetic life. Valerius commented upon Egeria's narrative and held her up as a model of holy pilgrimage for his monks to follow. In the course of his commentary the image of Egeria changed, and it was Valerius's narrative about Egeria that was included in the Escorial manuscript.

Valerius described Egeria's travels to the Holy Land, noting how she retraced the steps of the early Israelites and how, with fortitude, she climbed high holy mountains. Less interesting than Valerius's summary, however, is his commentary on her travels. Valerius offers Egeria as an example to his monks, challenging them to live up to the fortitude of this fragile woman. He then continues to praise her, saying that she mortified her body and made herself a pilgrim in this world in order that she might inherit the heavenly kingdom and join in the chorus of virgins. He then urges the brethren to be strong in their vigils, prayers and fasting so that they, too, may join Egeria in heaven.[23]

All Valerius's praise of Egeria's "mortification" and "fortitude" had no basis in her own narrative. She was no ascetic, yet through Valerius's account she became one, and as such she belonged in the codex of women who achieved independence and sanctity by adhering to an ascetic ideal of Christianity rather than a hierarchic one. To understand how Valerius could have so commented on her narrative, one must understand something about Valerius himself. Valerius was an ascetic holy man who had removed himself from society (made himself a "pilgrim to the world") in order to become closer to God. After he had acquired a reputation for sanctity by his austerities in the Spanish hills, Valerius became a monastic founder who always remained in some conflict with Church hierarchy, if only in his disdain for some priests.[24] He conformed to some degree to the older ascetic ideal of individualistic holy people reaching to God from outside established social structures. From this perspective, Valerius approached Egeria's writings and recognized elements he admired. The only things in the narrative that he could have identified as admirable were Egeria's status as a holy virgin and her pilgrimages, and what Valerius stressed were her travels. For Valerius, anyone who placed herself outside society, as Egeria had done, by her vow of chastity, and followed up such a vow by removing herself to holy spaces by pilgrimage, must by definition have been holy. Therefore, she qualified as a holy person. For Valerius, holy people must also fast and mortify their bodies, so he described Egeria in these terms in spite of the fact that the evidence within her narrative suggests that she was no ascetic. Egeria used her vow of chastity to justify freedom of movement throughout the Holy Land, but her pilgrimage earned her a reputation for sanctity through the writings of Valerius, despite contemporary criticism by Jerome.

Egeria ignored Jerome's caution to remain at home and not "visit the daughters of a strange land." In so doing, she not only established a degree of autonomy for herself but enhanced her reputation for sanctity among those who believed holy people should be separate from society, not part of a hierarchy of obedience.

Melania the Younger

A year after Egeria's return, in about 385, Melania was born into a rich Roman patrician family. She was probably of Spanish descent on her mother's side, and through her father she was related to some of the oldest and most powerful Roman families.[25] Not only had her family been influential politically, but some members had been in the forefront of the early Roman ascetic movement that had spread from the East. Melania's namesake and grandmother, Melania the Elder, had been an ascetic, a pilgrim, a monastic founder and an independent holy woman in her own right. Certainly the elder Melania exerted a great deal of influence on her granddaughter. The Life of Melania the Younger was written by Gerontius, who had been the priest serving Melania's monasteries and for whom Melania had been a spiritual mentor. It reveals the spiritual pilgrimage of Melania as she moved from the life of a pampered girl to that of a holy ascetic. The story unfolds against the background of the wealth of imperial Roman families, the vigor of early Eastern asceticism, and the drama of the barbarian invasions of the Empire. Melania's spiritual pilgrimage is dotted with actual pilgrimages as she moves both physically and spiritually from the Rome of her birth to her death in Jerusalem.

Gerontius tells us that from childhood Melania yearned for Christ and longed for bodily chastity. No doubt the example of her grandmother and other ascetic Roman women provided the model for the child's vision of a life other than the one expected of her. However, the demands of her patrician family required that she provide heirs. Therefore, when Melania was fourteen her family forced her to marry Pinian, a young man of a good family, if not as wealthy as her own. She begged Pinian to allow her to practice chastity within marriage. She even tried to buy her way out of the marriage debt by offering Pinian control of all her wealth, which was considerable, if he would only leave her virginity intact. She pleaded with him, saying: "... leave my body free so that I may bring it without stain along with my soul to Christ."[26] Pinian, however, wanted first to ensure the worldly succession of his family before considering the state of his soul, so he told Melania that she must bear two children before he would consider her request to be freed from carnality.

A daughter was duly born to the young couple and they promptly dedicated her to a life of virginity, no doubt at Melania's insistence. Melania again pleaded with Pinian to release her from the physical demands of marriage so that she might pursue spirituality, but he wanted to have one more child. At this point Melania considered escape, and indeed tried to flee the bonds of marriage by running away and leaving Pinian with all her possessions. She was dissuaded from her plan by certain "holy men" who suggested that she should stay and convert her husband to an ascetic life. Melania began to progress to sanctity by beginning ascetic practices. Gerontius tells us she began to wear a rough wool garment hidden under the soft silk clothing of the Roman upper classes. Melania always marked crucial turning points in her progress to spirituality by changing her clothing, and indeed this change from silk to wool marked a commitment to an asceticism that would free her from the gilded cage of matrimony.

Melania's strengthened resolve for an ascetic life continued even though she was once again pregnant. She did not care for herself during the pregnancy, and as the time of birth approached she kept an all-night vigil kneeling in her chapel. During this vigil, the Latin version of the Life demonstrates Melania's increasing independence by showing her in direct disobedience of her father. Her father was worried about his pregnant daughter's austerities and sent his eunuchs to her to be sure that she was resting. She bribed them to tell her father that she was reclining, but she stayed on her knees. This was the same kind of rebellion as wearing a wool shirt under silk. The young girl preserved the appearance of obedience while following her own will.

The austerities seem to have taken their toll, for the child was born prematurely. The infant boy died shortly after being baptized. Melania was ill after the delivery, and Pinian feared for her life. Melania told him that if he wanted her to survive he would have to vow that they would live perpetually chaste. Pinian granted Melania her wish and she was so cheered by his promise that she recovered completely. Once more Melania marked this step in spirituality by her choice of clothing. She renounced silk altogether and let the world see the rough wool which revealed her renunciation of her past life and the strength of her resolve. At about the same time their young daughter died, so there was nothing left to tie the couple to an earthly life. Even the objections of their parents ended with the death of Melania's father, and his deathbed acceptance of Melania's choice of an ascetic life.

Now the twenty-year-old woman was free to begin her ascetic pilgrimage in earnest, and the first thing she did was to move to the suburbs, away from the Roman center that had thus far shaped her life. Then she persuaded Pinian to wear simple clothing so that his outward

appearance would also express their growing spirituality. Pinian clearly
was not as eager for the ascetic life as Melania, for he changed to
clothing that was not as plain as Melania would have liked. However,
Melania corrected him and he proved receptive to her leadership in this
and in all subsequent decisions.

Melania and Pinian decided it would be wise to accustom themselves
slowly to the ascetic life, for as Melania observed, if they rushed into
extreme asceticism after their soft lives they would be much more liable
to fail. So they began their Christian lives by doing good works. They
visited the sick, distributed alms to the poor, and freed those who had
fallen into debt servitude. These early good works were part of the next
step in Melania's spiritual quest. After freeing herself from the carnal
demands of marriage, Melania sought to free herself from the immense
wealth that bound her to her past as well as to earthly responsibilities.
She herself said that the hardest part of the ascetic life was not struggling
against the flesh, but getting rid of all their wealth.[27] Indeed, given the
vast amount of wealth controlled by Melania and Pinian, it is under-
standable that it was very difficult for them to liquidate all of it. They
had property all over the Empire that they wanted to sell, and there were
thousands of slaves who would have to be sold or freed. Either option
would have a profound impact on the economy of Rome. Even beyond
this fixed property, they had movable goods too numerous to count, and
Pinian alone had an annual income of 120,000 pieces of gold.[28]

Melania appealed to the Empress Serena to help them liquidate the
property. Gerontius notes parenthetically that the Empress was duly
impressed by Melania's humble clothing,[29] the outward sign of her new
spiritual life. The Empress was moved by the plight of the young couple,
and said she would persuade Emperor Honorius to arrange for their
property to be sold through imperial agents and for the money to be
given to Melania and Pinian. This resolved some of the logistics of
getting poor, but problems still remained. For example, Melania's town
house was so valuable that no one in Rome, including the Emperor,
could afford to buy it. God did provide a solution for the expensive
house, as Gerontius explains somewhat nonchalantly: "The saints were
not able to sell the house, and after the invasion of the barbarians they
sold it for less than nothing since it was burned."[30]

Even as the property was being liquidated, Melania was faced with
getting rid of the gold that was acquired with each sale. The young
couple sent gold coins to holy men, founded monasteries, and even
bought islands for ascetics to use for withdrawing from society. The
barbarian invasions in the wake of which the couple fled to their African
properties provided other ways to spend their money. They ransomed
captives with the seemingly unending flow of gold. Throughout this

frantic divestment, Melania had nightmares about the amount of wealth she was trying to relinquish. Among other things, she dreamed that the Devil was accusing her of buying her way into heaven with the money she was using for charitable purposes. In spite of everything, the property slowly began to disappear. Gerontius noted the effect of this divestment on Melania: "The holy woman made advances in this virtue. She saw herself become a little lighter from the burden of possessions."[31]

After Melania had got rid of most of her possessions, she seems to have believed herself advanced to a higher degree of spirituality and ready for a more ascetic life. She began to fast, regularly escalating the degree until she ate only some moldy bread on Saturdays and Sundays.[32] She spent her days reading and writing. She knew both Latin and Greek, so many texts were accessible to her. The degree of independence Melania had acquired by her asceticism is indicated by Gerontius's noting that she alone decided what and how much she would read and write each day.[33] She lived as she pleased and chose for herself the activities that would best lead her to the spiritual life she sought. During this period, in addition to her studies, she began to assume a public role of teacher. She was such an advocate of chastity that she persuaded many people to follow this path. As was her custom, she marked this new public role by changing her clothing, making it more ascetic than it had been before. She changed from rough wool to a veil and hood made of haircloth, which she kept on constantly. People were astounded at this feat of deprivation, for they remembered the pampered, delicate child she used to be. As a child she could not tolerate even fine embroidery touching her skin, for it would cause an inflammation. Now she was wearing rough hair.

After leading this life for a few years, Melania decided again to escalate her asceticism by moving away from society. This was a pilgrimage in the tradition of desert fathers and mothers who withdrew to the fringes of society. Melania decided to live in a small cell and spend all her time praying and fasting, seeing no one.[34] However, she was already too well known to succeed in isolating herself from everyone. People continued to seek her out, so she had to schedule hours for visitors. Nevertheless, she did remove herself somewhat to strive for "even greater contests."[35]

After Melania and Pinian had lived in Africa for seven years they moved again. As Gerontius noted, "at last they left for Jerusalem to worship at the holy places."[36] Melania's spirituality was sufficiently advanced that she needed a new pilgrimage to enhance it further. Their ship sailed eastward and stopped for a time at Alexandria. There they met well-known holy men and one of them, the holy father Nestoros, saw the couple in a crowd and recognized their holiness. Given Melania's hair shirt and hood, this recognition was probably not as miraculous as Gerontius would have us think. This incident did show, however, that the kind of asceticism Melania was practicing was not intended to be a private one.

Finally they reached Jerusalem where Melania once again resumed a life of fasting, study and conversation with bishops and other theologians. During this period, she lived alone with her mother. The Life says that Pinian, too, was in Jerusalem, but it is not clear exactly where he was living. Melania seems to have been successful at giving away her wealth, because she was very poor in Jerusalem. While her poverty pleased her immensely, she seemed not unhappy at a sudden windfall that came to her.

Some of the couple's Spanish properties that had never been sold because of the barbarian invasions were finally liquidated. The gold was delivered to the holy couple in Jerusalem, and Melania accepted it eagerly. With this new gold, she immediately decided it was time to travel again, and suggested to Pinian that they go to Egypt and visit the holy men and women there. Pinian docilely agreed, so the couple set off. They toured the deserts of Egypt, which were inhabited by holy men and virgins. While they were there, Melania once again impoverished the couple by hiding their gold in the cells of holy people who did not want it. Then they went to Alexandria to talk to other holy bishops and abbots. Finally, before completing their tour, they went south to Nitria, where there was a large community of holy people. From there they visited the cells where hermits lived. There Melania was received by the holy men "as if she were a man."[37] In fact, by her asceticism and her pilgrimages Melania had transcended the traditional expectations of women's roles.

Melania and Pinian were now ready to return to Jerusalem. Once again they had no money, but they were "weighted down with a full load of piety"[38] conveyed to them by their pilgrimage to the living holy men and women of the desert. After returning from this pilgrimage, Melania retired to a small cell on the Mount of Olives. There she received only a few visitors and lived an ascetic life. This way of life seems to have been modeled on that of the desert fathers and mothers she saw in Egypt. After fifteen years, Melania decided to build a monastery and surround herself with other women. A movement from an eremetic to a coenobitic life was not an uncommon pattern for holy people. Melania surrounded herself with ninety virgins, as well as some reformed prostitutes, to form a community.

During this coenobitic period of Melania's life, Pinian died, and Melania arranged for a monastery for men to be built in his honor. It would seem at this point that Melania had completed her pilgrimages. She was an acknowledged holy woman, free to do as she pleased and follow her conscience with regard to her spiritual development. She had also made the requisite pilgrimages, having traveled to the holy places as well as to the deserts populated with holy people. Now she was settled in a monastery. However, Melania did not give up her desire to travel. As soon as an opportunity presented itself, she was ready to leave again. There can be no doubt that she enjoyed her travels, and since she was such an acknowledged holy person, each of her trips took on the aspect of a pilgrimage, a holy journey.

Melania heard that her uncle, Volusian, was going to visit Constantinople from the west. She was anxious to see him and decided to visit Constantinople to meet with him. Volusian was a pagan, so Melania had a spiritual motive for the journey. She would convert him from his paganism to Christianity. There was obviously some controversy as to the legitimacy of this trip. The discomfort that emerges from the Life may stem either from Melania's recognition that this much travel was not deemed appropriate for holy women, or from Gerontius's knowledge of the degree to which such travel was forbidden by Church Fathers. In any case, Gerontius said that Melania "struggled mightily" with the question of her departure, but then decided to leave. Perhaps to vindicate the trip, the Life describes a miracle that took place along the way. Apparently, there was some difficulty in the journey because the group did not have the appropriate travel documents for all their animals. At a crucial moment, an official recognized Melania and released the animals. Melania concluded from this incident that the "journey is in accordance with God's will."[39] As miracles go, this one is pretty small. It seems that the hagiographer was going out of his way to justify Melania's love of travel and the freedom to do so that her status as holy woman provided.

The saint's visit in Constantinople was a huge success. She was well received by everyone and enjoyed talking theology from "dawn to dusk."[40] She also persuaded her uncle to convert, even though he had expressed dismay at seeing her in such shabby clothing. Melania returned to Jerusalem in time to celebrate Easter at the sacred places, then she resumed her coenobitic life.

Melania had hardly returned to her settled existence before another opportunity to travel presented itself. The Empress Eudocia, who had entertained Melania graciously in Constantinople, decided to make a pilgrimage to the holy places. Melania wrestled once more with the correctness of another departure and, not surprisingly, decided to go and meet the Empress. The two women traveled together, enjoying a close companionship, for Gerontius explained that they were "strongly bonded in a spiritual love."[41] As always, Melania performed miracles on this journey, no doubt justifying the trip as well as enhancing her reputation for sanctity.

Finally, Melania finished her tour of the holy places, culminating at Bethlehem. There she predicted her final pilgrimage, her death. She then returned to her monastery in Jerusalem to prepare for her last spiritual journey. Melania said goodbye to her nuns, giving them final advice. At this point the Latin manuscript contains an anecdote absent from the manuscripts of the Greek tradition. In this story, the Empress Eudocia sent for some of Melania's virgins to come out of the monastery to visit her. Melania appeared in a vision to warn the nuns and Eudocia against this proposed flight from enclosure. In the narrative, Eudocia repented and sent the nuns back to their monastery.[42]

This incident presents a strong statement in favor of enclosure that is remarkably inconsistent with the facts of Melania's life, which was full of travel. Pilgrimages marked the significant points in her pathway to sanctity, and pilgrimages were exceeded in importance only by chastity as a value Melania held. It seems highly improbable that her virtual last words to the women she cared for were that they should stay enclosed. I believe this incident was added to the Latin manuscript at some point early in its transmission as an attempt to bring the *Vita* of this saintly and influential woman in line with patristic prescriptions of enclosure for women.[43] The very fact that someone felt compelled to add such an incident to the end of Melania's life argues for the striking degree of freedom of movement that was exemplified in this holy woman's career. Enclosure was something to which Melania retreated periodically, not an ideal. She represented a tradition for ascetic women which the Church Fathers would not have accepted.

The narrative of the Life continues to the saint's death. After bidding her final goodbyes to the monks, priests and other visitors, she entrusted the care of her monasteries to Gerontius, the faithful priest who wrote her *Vita*. Then, with a communion wafer on her lips,[44] Melania died. Gerontius carefully described what she wore as she was buried: "clothing worthy of her sanctity."[45] So dressed, Melania completed her final pilgrimage: to join the angels in heaven, whose "passionlessness she had imitated on earth."[46]

The Life of Melania contains many elements that are important in understanding the view of sexuality and womanhood implicit in these stories. Her companionship with other women, like Egeria's, will remain a theme throughout these Lives, as will Melania's desire to proclaim her asceticism publicly by being concerned about the clothing she wore. These and other themes will be discussed more fully in the final chapter; here it is important to highlight the degree to which freedom of travel came with female asceticism in the minds of these two women; they did not want to be enclosed within walls erected by patristic prescription. In their pilgrimages, Melania and Egeria had much in common. Both achieved the freedom to travel by their vows of virginity, which put them outside the normal constraints of women. They both went to the same locations and sought sanctity by geography. Furthermore, they both enjoyed their traveling and sought it out beyond the basic pilgrimages. There was a significant difference between them, however. Over and above her pilgrimages, Melania was an ascetic holy woman in her own right. The distinction between the two is important because it suggests that Melania did not earn freedom to travel by her ascetic practices, but by her vow of virginity that put her outside the usual constraints of women. Egeria shared that status, and she, too, could be free to travel, even if her travels did not demonstrate any particularly harsh asceticisms. Other women went even further than Egeria and Melania, not satisfied with escaping the recommendation of enclosure suggested to aspiring holy women. Some women dressed as men in order not only to escape the constraints placed on women, but to escape their gender completely.

7

Freedom from Gender Identification
Pelagia and Castissima

> Others change their garb and assume the
> mien of men ... (Jerome[1])

All the women in the previous chapters used their vows of chastity to transcend the gender requirements and expectations that might have shaped their lives. In each of these Lives, women expressed their independence in a number of different ways. This chapter will explore the culmination of women transcending such social expectations. These women used their vows to escape completely their identification as women and to enter the world of men. Mary of Egypt almost escaped gender identification because her ascetic deprivations made Zosimas not recognize her as a woman, in spite of her nakedness, until she identified herself and asked for his cloak. This incident perhaps introduces the possibility that women could completely transcend their gender.

There is a tradition of saints' lives in which women, upon their conversion to chastity, dress in men's clothes and live as men either in the world or in a monastery. The earliest example of this is in the apocryphal Acts of Paul and Thecla, in which Thecla dressed as a man to join Paul in his mission.[2] An even more dramatic example of the symbolic transformation of gender may be found in the early Life of Perpetua, in which Perpetua in a dream saw herself borne into the amphitheater, stripped of her clothes, and changed into a man. Building on this early tradition, numbers of such women are described in a genre popular throughout the Middle Ages all over Europe.

Under the system of the early Fathers that identified women as carnal, this should have been a desirable option. Logically, the complete transcendence of the carnal would have converted sexual women into spiritual men. The Fathers, however, were as unwilling to support such a radical transformation as they were to support women transcending even the social expectations which bound them. In a seeming exception, Ambrose described an incident in which he spoke approvingly of a woman dressing as a man. In his narrative, a Christian virgin was condemned to a house of prostitution. A soldier took pity on her and, before she was defiled, offered to change clothes with her and let her escape in the guise of a soldier while he remained dressed in her clothes to surprise the next patron. The ruse worked; the virgin escaped and ultimately both received their reward by a joint martyrdom. Ambrose seems to have approved of this cross-dressing, for he relates the tale as an exemplum in his tract "Concerning Virgins." Furthermore, he has the surprised second patron of the whorehouse express the miraculous (if not strictly accurate) sense of the incident by saying: "I had heard but believed not that Christ changed water into wine; now He has begun also to change the sexes."[3]

Ambrose's description of this event might suggest that the Fathers could approve of the transformation of woman into spiritual man. That was not the case, however. The transformation of the sexes was sufficiently threatening to the social order for the Fathers to disapprove of it. Even Ambrose concurred in this, carefully quoting the biblical prohibition forbidding cross-dressing and saying: "... what nature herself abhors must be unsuitable. ... Nature clothes each sex in its proper raiment."[4] Apparently, what Ambrose found acceptable about the incident he praised was that the woman did not choose the transformation. The initiative for it came from the soldier; thus at least the virgin kept her natural role of passive woman. That principle would have been violated had she chosen to take on the male disguise on her own initiative.

Jerome, too, disapproved of the practice of cross-dressing, forbidding Eustochium even to associate with women who had assumed men's clothing. The recommendation against such practices found its way into Church law at the early-fourth-century Council of Gangra, which forbade either sex to adopt the clothing of the other.[5] This prohibition is consistent with other, more general, patristic discussions on the subject. After all, if Tertullian were offended at the idea that virgins were not women, he could hardly approve of them passing as men. Women could aspire to spirituality, but should not aspire to escape the general social requirements that bound them in their gender roles. They could be spiritual women, but always slightly inferior to spiritual men. However, just as some women did not accept patristic prohibition against other activities, some did not accept the ban against forsaking their identification as women. Two such women, Pelagia and Castissima, are represented in the Escorial manuscript.

Pelagia

Pelagia was a beautiful prostitute who lived in Antioch in the fifth century. She died about 457 and a cult for her existed as early as 530. The Life was written by Jacob the Deacon, who claimed to have witnessed the events he described. Jacob calls on all listeners to hear his tale of a splendid repentance.[6]

The story began when the Bishop of Antioch convened a council of eight bishops. Among those summoned was Bishop Nonnus, who can probably be identified as the Bishop of Edessa who lived c. 451. Nonnus came to the council accompanied by his deacon, Jacob, author of this narrative. The bishops convened and met at the basilica of the Blessed Julian the Martyr.[7] They gathered in the forecourt of the church and listened to Bishop Nonnus speak. All were educated by his words, which were enunciated with the aid of the Holy Spirit.

Suddenly, a beautiful woman appeared riding on an ass. She was so elaborately ornamented that nothing could be seen on her but gold and pearls and precious stones. With her came a train of young men and women clad in rich robes with torques of gold about their necks. The very air was scented with rich perfumes as she passed by. Upon seeing this impudent woman who rode with not even a veil to cover her head, and did not descend from her ass for the honor of God or His representatives, the bishops turned their faces away as from a grievous sin. But Bishop Nonnus did not turn his head; he gazed at her long and carefully.

After the woman had passed, Nonnus fell to his knees and shed many tears. Sighing heavily, he asked the other bishops: "Did not the beauty of the woman delight you?"[8] The bishops did not answer him, but Nonnus was not deterred. He said again: "In truth, it greatly delighted me, and well pleased was I with her beauty." The other bishops still did not answer, but Nonnus continued, much inspired by the beauty of the prostitute. He noted the time the woman spent adorning herself so that there would be no stain or flaw in her body's beauty. Thus, she was careful to please all men's eyes and not disappoint her earthly lovers. In contrast, Nonnus felt that they were trying to please God, an immortal Lover, and they could not clean their souls nor make them nearly as beautiful as the prostitute's body.

With this vision, Nonnus took his deacon and retreated to his cell, where he continued his lamentations: "Lord Christ, have mercy on a sinner, for a single day's adorning of a prostitute is far beyond the adorning of my soul. ... She has promised to please men, and has kept her word. I have promised to please God, and have lied. ..."[9] The impact of the vision of the prostitute's beauty on Nonnus is quite remarkable. In all the patristic writings, the Fathers warned that the mere vision of any woman could lead a man to sin. In this case, the vision of a beautiful fallen woman led a bishop not to sin, but to a recognition that he was imperfect. In fact, the vision of a prostitute inspired the saintly Bishop to a higher recognition of holiness. This is a reversal of the standard expectations of patristic warnings against looking at women.

Nonnus's sentiments seemed to be given divine validation by a dream that came to him after his recognition that his soul compared unfavorably with the prostitute's body. He described his dream to his deacon:

> I was standing near the horns of the altar when a black dove kept flying over me. It was filthy and stank. After the congregation had departed, the dove approached again. I stretched out my hand, caught the dove and plunged it into the holy water of the church. There it was made clean and the foul smell that had accompanied it disappeared. The dove emerged from the water as white as snow and flew up to heaven where my eyes could no longer follow it.[10]

After describing this reassuring dream to his deacon, the Bishop proceeded to the church to meet with other churchmen. They went to the city's largest church, where Nonnus was asked to speak. When he had received the appropriate permission to preach, Nonnus began to speak, full of inspiration from the Holy Spirit. The congregation was so moved by his words that the floor of the church was made wet with their tears. Now, it so happened that by divine guidance, the prostitute who had so moved the Bishop was in the congregation. She, who had never before thought of sin, was moved to tears by his words. She commanded two of her servants to remain and discover where Nonnus was staying. The young men followed the Bishop and deacon and discovered that they were staying at the basilica of the Blessed Julian the Martyr. The prostitute sent a letter to Bishop Nonnus asking that he grant her an audience.

Bishop Nonnus responded that he would be pleased to see her to instruct her in divine things. However, he further said that he was a man and subject to temptation, so he would not see her alone, but only in the presence of the other bishops. This is an interesting acknowledgement of his human frailty. On the one hand, it draws from the traditional view of the hazards of associating with women. On a deeper level, however, it calls into question the degree to which Nonnus's first view of the prostitute really caused him to think only of God. Much of his prayer and lamentation and feelings of inadequacy probably arose because in reality he was drawn to her carnal beauty as much as to her spiritual potential.

In any case, the prostitute came to the church filled with joy. Nonnus called the other bishops together and received the woman. She threw herself at his feet, saying she wanted to become a Christian and be baptized. All the bishops were moved to tears by the repentance of the beautiful woman, but Nonnus said the laws of the Church required that no prostitute should be baptized unless someone were willing to provide surety that she would not fall back into her old sins. The woman was impatient to be saved and challenged the Bishop, saying: "You shall answer to God for my soul, and if you delay to baptize me, I shall charge all my evil deeds to you. ... May you deny God and worship idols if you do not this day make me born again and a bride to Christ."[11] All present were astounded at this brave speech and at the deep desire for salvation shown by the harlot. The speech is certainly one of a woman who is used to having her own way, and in this she was persuasive. The deacon Jacob was sent to the Bishop of the city to get his permission for the baptism. He returned promptly, accompanied by a deaconess to assist in the ceremony.

In preparation for the baptism, the Bishop asked the prostitute her name. She answered him: "At birth the name I received was Pelagia. However, the townspeople of Antioch call me Margarite, because of the pearls with which I was adorned from the Devil's work." Then the Bishop asked her: "Your own name is Pelagia?" She answered: "Yes, my lord." He then baptized her Pelagia, and the deaconess, Romana, stood as her godmother. Bishop Nonnus announced that in celebration they would eat extra oil in their food and drink wine with spiritual joy.[12]

The question of the woman's name appears at this critical and most dramatic point in the narrative: the moment of her baptism, her rebirth. Before this moment, she is not named; she remains an anonymous and, indeed, almost a stereotypical prostitute. It did not matter who she was; what mattered was what she was. At the moment of her baptism, we are told not only who she is but that she has two identities: her original identity, represented by the name given at her birth, Pelagia; and her sinful identity, represented by the name Margarite. This dual identity in some ways forecasts an additional identity change that will come later in the Life. Of additional interest is the meaning of the names. Pelagia means belonging to the sea, and Margarite means pearl – referring, as she said, to the pearls that decorated her during her sinful life. Now, the relationship between these two names is obvious. As pearls are from the sea, the woman was not fundamentally changed when she entered into her life of sin. Even more surprising than the complementary nature of the two names is the choice of "Margarite" as the name of the prostitute. Pearls were associated with purity and virginity,[13] so to call the prostitute "Pearl" seems unusual at best. Yet it suggests that the woman had a virtue even while she was living as a prostitute. There must have been an innate purity that was unaffected by her occupation. Perhaps it was this pearl of purity that the Bishop saw when he was driven to prayer by the woman's beauty.

The view of sexuality portrayed in this Life is much more generous than any discussed in the patristic work. Referring to the prostitute as a "pearl" even after she had fallen seems to contradict the spirit of Jerome, for example, when he says: "... though God can do all things he cannot raise up a virgin when she has fallen."[14] Pelagia not only does not lose all possibility for regeneration, but even while she is indulging herself carnally she does not lose the attributes of the pearl. After her baptism she reassumes her original name, but since it means belonging to the sea, she can retain the pearl-like purity.

Understandably, Pelagia's baptism did not please the Devil, who appeared pounding at the door just as everyone was seated at the celebratory meal. He cried and lamented, reprimanding Nonnus for taking his prize. He also accused Pelagia of being like Judas and deserting her master. The Bishop was unaffected by the diabolic presence, and just told Pelagia to sign herself with the Cross and thus renounce the Devil. She did so and breathed upon the demon, who then disappeared. However, the Devil did not so easily give up his beautiful follower. Two days later, when Pelagia was asleep with her godmother, the Devil reappeared, wakened God's handmaid, and tried to tempt her to her previous life. He said: "Tell me, my lady Margarite, what I did to displease you. Were you not decorated in precious stones and pearls? Were you not covered in gold and silver? Tell me what more I can do for you, but do not permit the Christians to mock me."[15] Pelagia crossed herself and breathed on the Devil, again making him vanish.

Pelagia demonstrated that the Devil's temptations did not move her. The next day she called her servant and told him to go to her home and list everything of value. She then turned all her riches over to Bishop Nonnus, asking him to dispose of the wealth she had earned in her previous sinful life. Nonnus turned all the wealth over to the treasurer of the church, stipulating that none of it should be used to enrich the church itself, but all should go to widows, orphans and the poor. Thus Pelagia progressed in sanctity.

On the eighth day she was expected to put off her white robes of baptism and dress as a Christian woman. Instead, she rose by night without anyone knowing, laid aside her white robes and put on the tunic and cloak of Bishop Nonnus. She disappeared into the night and was not seen again in the city of Antioch. Pelagia rejected the role that was expected of her: to become a Christian woman. Instead, she chose to become as much like her mentor as possible. She took his clothes, and with his clothes assumed the identity of a man. Not only had she renounced her previous life and changed her name, she renounced her gender altogether.

Her godmother, Romana, wept at the woman's disappearance, but Nonnus consoled her, saying: "Weep not, daughter, but rejoice rather with great joy, for Pelagia has chosen the better part, even as Mary, whom the Lord put before Martha in the Gospel."[16] Nonnus was here approving of Pelagia's rejection of her role as a woman, just as Mary had rejected traditional woman's work to listen to Christ. Some time after this, the Bishop of Antioch summoned all the visiting bishops to dismiss them and let them return to their own cities. Nonnus and his deacon, Jacob, returned to their city.

Three or four years later, Jacob longed to go on a pilgrimage to Jerusalem. He asked his bishop for permission to leave. Permission was granted, and in addition, the Bishop advised Jacob to inquire in Jerusalem about a certain holy man named Pelagius, who was a monk and a eunuch with a reputation for much holiness. Jacob might profit from a visit with the holy eunuch. Jacob, the narrator, advises us that "all the time he spoke of God's handmaid Pelagia, but I knew it not."[17] The identification of Pelagius as a eunuch on the one hand is a fairly practical designation. If a woman were to pass as a man for any length of time, it would have been credible only if all believed he were a eunuch. On another level, the designation of eunuch reveals what Pelagia had accomplished: she was now asexual. She did not dress as a man to become a man, with a man's frailties and desires. By dressing as a man she not only transcended her own gender, she transcended both genders. She was an asexual eunuch for Christ.

Jacob worshipped at the holy places in Jerusalem, then inquired after the servant of God. He found Pelagius in a cell on the Mount of Olives. (This means that Pelagia would have had a cell in the same location, and at about the same time, as Melania the Younger.[18]) Jacob approached the cell of the holy eunuch and knocked on the shutter of the small window. She recognized the deacon, but as he wrote, "I knew her not. How could I know her, when she whom I had seen before in beauty beyond all telling was thin and gaunt from fasting?"[19] They prayed together and Jacob left, much improved by the visit. He continued his travels for a while, but longed to return to the Mount of Olives to visit once again with Pelagius.

Upon his return, there was no response to his knock on the cell. Looking into the cell, Jacob saw that Pelagius was dead. He returned to Jerusalem to tell everyone of the death of this very holy man. When the other monks began to prepare the body for burial, they discovered that Pelagius was a woman. Jacob then knew who the holy eunuch really was. Everyone was amazed at the miracle, saying: "Glory to you, God

who has many saints hidden on earth."[20] Many people came to attend
the burial, and the holy body was buried with great honor.

Jacob concluded the Life, saying that he faithfully recorded all the
events. As proof, he said, "anyone who goes to the holy places may
inquire about the monk Pelagius." Here, near the end of his narrative,
Jacob referred to her as Pelagius, the masculine name. The transformation of her gender outlasted the discovery of the secret at her death.
The manuscript section ends with the words: "Here ends the life of Saint
Pelagia who before was called Margarite."

Castissima

The Life of the virgin Castissima in the Escorial manuscript is essentially
the same narrative as that of the Eastern saint, Euphrosyne.[21] When the
Life was brought to Spain from the East and translated into Latin, the
translator must have changed the name of the virgin to make it more
symbolically accessible to the Latin audience. The original name,
Euphrosyne, is the name of one of the three Graces, representing chaste
joy. The Latin-derived name, Castissima, more directly calls forth
associations of chastity and purity for a Latin audience. In the manipu-
lation of the name, however, the hagiographer indicates that this is going
to be a narrative in which identity is a significant fact, just as it was in the
Life of Pelagia.

The narrative begins in the city of Alexandria in the home of a God-
fearing couple, Paphnutius and his wife. They were wealthy, pious and
content in all respects except one: the wife was barren and they very
much wanted a child. They prayed, gave great wealth to the poor and
sick, and did all they could to achieve their desire. At last they visited a
certain monastery in which lived a pious abbot. The abbot joined his
prayers to theirs, and God took pity on the couple and granted them one
daughter, whom they named Castissima. Her parents took much joy in
her.

When she was twelve years old, Castissima's mother died. The girl's
father took over the task of educating her, and taught her much of scriptures and the wisdom of God. She was quick to learn, and her father was
proud of her. Her name was spread throughout the city because of her
wisdom, her love of learning, and her great beauty. Of course, many
important men sought to acquire her as a bride for their sons. One of
these men, who stood above all the others in power, succeeded in persuading Castissima's father to betroth her to his son. The betrothal
presents were exchanged, binding the agreement.

A short time after the betrothal agreement, when Castissima was eighteen, her father took her to visit the monastery where years before he had prayed for his daughter's conception. While father and daughter stayed at the monastery, the girl heard the abbot speak of purity and virginity and the fear of God. During this visit, she progressed greatly in wisdom. She observed the spiritual life of the monks and said to herself: "Blessed are all who live in this place. They are like angels who praise God without ceasing. And after death they will be worthy of eternal life."[22] She began to repent in her heart of the life that was chosen for her. The monastery that had brought about her birth triggered her rebirth into a chaste life. After the three-day visit, Paphnutius was ready to leave with his daughter. He asked the abbot's blessing for the girl, received it and left.

Some time later, the abbot sent one of the brothers to bring Paphnutius to the monastery for a celebration. The brother found only Castissima at home, and she eagerly questioned him about life in the monastery. His answers made her long for the monastic life, but she was afraid her father would never permit her to renounce the world. The monk encouraged her desire for an ascetic life, saying: "No, my daughter, do not give your body up into corruption, nor surrender your beauty to shameful passion, but be whole in your purity as a bride of Christ, who will give you the kingdom of heaven. Run and hide; join a monastery and there you will be saved." Curiously, Castissima expressed only one reservation about this plan to run and hide in a monastery: "Who will tonsure me? For I do not wish to be shaved by a layman, but by a servant of God."[23]

Here, the focus of Castissima's transformation from woman to eunuch of God lies in the cutting of her hair. A woman's hair was a symbol and an expression of her sexuality and her gender. That was why the Fathers always advocated that women and virgins should veil their heads. To cut her hair would mark a dramatic renunciation of Castissima's previous existence. Her insistence that it be done by a servant of God no doubt emphasizes the fact that it was being done for the highest spiritual motives. There was reason for the hagiographer to insist that the tonsuring was spiritual, for not only had Fathers like Jerome and Tertullian disapproved of women cutting their hair, but in AD 390 a law was passed that forbade such tonsuring. The mandate of Valentinian II said: "Women who shall have shorn their hair contrary to divine and human laws ... should be debarred from the doors of a church."[24] By focusing on the dramatic element of cutting her hair, Castissima's hagiographer was highlighting the degree to which such transformations violated the customs that ordered society.

The monk suggested that while he took Paphnutius to the monastery, Castissima could send for another monk to come and tonsure her. This was accomplished: an old recluse came, shaved the girl's head, dressed her in a woman's robe suitable for a penitent, and departed. Castissima then considered her situation. She said to herself: "If I go to a monastery of women, my father will never cease to look for me until I am found, and he will take me away by force to be given to my betrothed. Instead, I will put myself in a monastery of men in the disguise of a eunuch and no one will suspect me."[25] When it was evening, she took off her women's clothes, dressed herself in the clothing of a man, and left her house, taking five hundred solidi with her.

In this incident, the tonsuring was accomplished with the sanction of a holy man, but the final transformation of virgin to eunuch was done solely at her own initiative. The excuse she gave for the final transformation seems implausible. Her father is depicted in the Life as a pious, indulgent parent, and it would seem out of character for him to force his daughter to marry. Instead, the girl seemed to want to seek a higher spirituality, a transformation of self in addition to a renunciation of the world.

Castissima went to the monastery that had played such a continuing role in her life. She presented herself to the porter, saying: "Brother, please go and tell the abbot that a certain eunuch from the palace is at the door and wants to speak to him."[26] Castissima has presented herself as a eunuch: her sexual renunciation and transformation are complete. Just as with Pelagia, the change in identity required a name change as well. When the abbot accepted the eunuch into the monastery (accepting the 500 solidi as payment), he asked the young man's name. "Emerald," replied the youth. Emeralds were known to symbolize faith, purity and the ability to overcome trials and sin,[27] all qualities of the disguised Castissima. The abbot accepted Emerald into the monastery and placed him in the care of Agapius, an older monk who would serve as his guide and mentor, saying: "Let this man be henceforth your son and disciple."[28] Agapius became like a father to replace the one the girl had left.

However, when the eunuch joined the monastic community, a problem arose. Upon Emerald's entrance into the refectory, "Satan made many to stumble at his beauty."[29] The youth was so fair of face that the monks were tempted, so the abbot sent Emerald to live in a separate cell away from the monastery proper. There the youth could sing hymns, eat, and be tutored by Agapius. This incident seems to point out how superior was Emerald's state even to that of the other monks. She had truly become an asexual eunuch for God; it was not she who was tempted. The monks, however, were still prey to the frailties of carnal flesh; they could be drawn to a beautiful eunuch. Emerald peacefully withdrew to the cell and began a life of such zealous piety that all were astounded.

Meanwhile, Paphnutius discovered that his daughter had gone. He searched for her and lamented her loss. The whole city mourned the absence of the young girl. In his despair, Paphnutius went to the monastery to seek the prayers of the holy men to aid him in his search. All the monks prayed that the whereabouts of the lost girl might be revealed to the father, but their prayers were to no avail, because the prayers of Emerald "overcame the prayers and vigils of all the brethren."[30] Again, the eunuch's spirituality is portrayed as superior to that of all the monks. The abbot tried to console the father by saying that since God did not reveal the location of the lost girl, she must be devoted to a good cause. Somewhat consoled, Paphnutius returned home.

The next time the father visited the monastery, the abbot suggested that the old man might profit from a visit with their pious recluse, Emerald. Paphnutius did not recognize his daughter, as she was so changed by much fasting and other austerities. However, the two had such a wonderful talk that Paphnutius praised the eunuch to the abbot, saying: "How much have I profited from this man. God knows how my soul has been captured by his love, as if he had been my own daughter."[31]

After Emerald had been in the monastery for thirty-eight years, she fell ill. During this illness, Paphnutius arrived at the monastery for one of his periodic visits. He visited the sick monk for the last time and begged his prayers, asking that he be released from the grief about his missing daughter. Emerald assured him that soon he would have information about the lost Castissima. The father waited three days with the sick monk. On the third day, Emerald knew she was dying and revealed herself to Paphnutius: "My father, ... end your grief for Castissima your daughter. I am she."[32] After she had spoken, she yielded up her spirit to God. Agapius saw Paphnutius mourning his dead daughter and ran weeping to the abbot. When all the monks heard how the woman had lived among them all those years as a eunuch, they were amazed and sang praises to God who had wrought such miracles.

At the funeral one of the monks, who was blind in one eye, stepped up to embrace the body, and immediately the sight in his eye was restored. The monks who witnessed this miracle saw it as God's approval of "... those who are willing to take refuge in the love of our Lord Jesus Christ."[33] The miracle does justify Castissima's choice to live her life as the eunuch Emerald, but it perhaps reveals more. As the blind man was permitted to see at the death of the saint, all the monks who had been blind to the presence of the woman saw the truth at her death. The choice of the name Emerald reinforces the symbolism that she brings vision, and in turn truth. Emeralds were believed to cure eye diseases,[34] so the metaphor was made actual in the miracle of the curing.

The strong suggestion here is that the girl, Chastity (Castissima), became a eunuch, Emerald, to bring a revealed truth to the faithful, to open their eyes to a reality of faith. This reality of faith may have been obvious to the medieval holy people who were treasuring the narratives of such transvestite saints, but it is somewhat obscure to the twentieth-century reader. The existence of a number of saints' lives in which women dress as men has intrigued scholars, and generated some controversy.

Hermann Usener, writing in the nineteenth century, saw the origins of such transvestite saints in the old pagan worship of the bisexual Aphroditos of Cyprus, to whom women sacrificed while dressed in men's clothing, and men worshipped in women's clothing.[35] This view virtually prevailed for a century until Marie Delcourt argued that the practice was not simply a holdover from paganism, but grew from impulses within the Roman Christian world. She saw the prototype of the transvestite saint not in Aphroditos of Cyprus, but rather in the story of St Thecla. This story was preserved in the Apocryphal Acts of Paul and Thecla and this comes from the ascetic tradition that produced much of the literature describing women using Christian chastity to establish personal sovereignty. Delcourt saw the change of clothing by women in these stories as symbolic of breaking away from their feminine past and a refusal to accept organized established order.[36]

Delcourt's argument makes sense. The Lives of the transvestite saints in the Escorial manuscript represent the logical conclusion of all the Lives in this collection, just as these saints represent the highest achievement of women in the ascetic tradition. The women described in the previous chapters used religious chastity to escape the requirements imposed upon their gender. Pelagia and Castissima used religious chastity to escape their gender altogether. These Lives are an expression of strong, independent ascetic women. However, this explanation of the popularity of this type of Life is insufficient. It explains why certain women might be drawn to such narratives, but does not explain their wide popularity with both men and women. Monks copied and preserved these stories just as women did.

John Anson has attempted to explain the attraction of such stories to monks. He, too, saw the origin of the transvestite theme in the Thecla story, and then argued that it was sustained and developed in the monasteries of Scetis.[37] He believed these stories to be a product of monks' fears of women and of sexual temptation: "Thus, quite simply, the secret longing for a woman in a monastery is brilliantly concealed by disguising the woman as a man. ..."[38] So, men longing to have a woman near them created a story in which a non-threatening woman resides in their community, and Anson argued that "her disguise rescues the community by warding off demonic femininity, by rendering finally harmless the threatening vision of woman."[39] While this argument has some merit, there are two problems. First of all, Anson's theory does not take into account the strong and rebellious nature of the women involved. If they were created to be non-threatening to the monastic community, the Lives would not include the message of strong feminine independence that is so much a part of these stories. In fact, such independence would be counterproductive to a moral of passive, harmless womanhood. Furthermore, the Thecla story, if it is the prototype of subsequent ones, had nothing to do with a monastic community. Thecla dressed as a man to wander and preach, not to live harmoniously in a monastery. It seems that Anson cannot argue both that Thecla was the prototype and that the stories were products of monastic fearful longings.

Wayne Meeks presented a more complex explanation for the popularity of the transvestite stories. He argued that since the stories began in the Gnostic ascetic tradition revealed in the Apocryphal Acts, their symbolism must be understood in the Gnostic tradition which had a highly developed myth of the virtue of the androgyne. Meeks said that in this tradition, "the union of male and female represents not a heightened or even a spiritualized libido, but a neutralization of sexuality, and therefore a renunciation of all ties which join the 'unified' individual with society."[40] He essentially argued that when women cross-dressed in the Lives they did not become men, they became androgynes, embodying the principles of both male and female; this neutralized their gender, making them asexual. Furthermore, this new asexual being would be so complete that he/she would need none of the social structures that supported and completed imperfect sexual beings. Indeed, the androgyne is exempt from social structures. This theory explains why men would find stories of transvestite women appealing: these women represented an androgynous ideal of asexuality that was central to ascetic Christianity of both genders. It is significant to note, however, that men did not cross-dress.[41] Therefore, it cannot be only that these transvestite Lives are explained as representing people's yearnings for an androgynous state. If so, the model of a man cross-dressing would have been equally popular. Meeks's hypothesis is suggestive, but not sufficient.

To understand these Lives, one needs to begin with the recognition that they yielded a metaphoric reality that appealed to both male and female ascetics. The Lives state that by cross-dressing, a woman becomes a eunuch. If we take the language of the Lives at face value, then the women did not become androgynes, as Meeks suggested. A eunuch was asexual not by virtue of adding the opposite gender, but by removing his sexuality; he was a man with the troublesome carnality eliminated. The monks residing in the monasteries were also striving to become eunuchs for God. The Church forbade them to become physical eunuchs; they had to struggle to attain asexuality through will. By becoming metaphorically asexual, the transvestite women became what the monks aspired to be. So, as he listened to these Lives, each monk could imagine himself to be as innocent of sex as the disguised woman. He could hope that at his death, he too would be revealed as human and all would marvel at how he had been able to maintain asexuality throughout his life, just as all marveled at the eunuchs who were revealed as women. So, on the one hand, these stories are about the escape from carnality. In this way, they appealed to men of the ascetic tradition.

On the other hand, the women who cross-dressed were making an additional statement by their actions: they were renouncing expected behavior. Even after she had converted to chastity, Pelagia was expected to wear the clothing and live the life of a normal Christian woman. She rejected this in favor of a more dramatic transformation: to become a eunuch for God. So while a monk might see the role of eunuch as the role he is expected to fulfill, the women who acted on this lifestyle or simply admired it incorporated a rejection of the established order and expectations. To become a eunuch for God and live in a monastery was expected for a pious monk; it was revolutionary for a woman. These Lives bring into focus the difference between the ascetic ideal for men and for women. Both could aspire to the highest goal of asexual Christianity, but women took this a step farther and used asexual Christianity to escape their social, and indeed their biological, destiny.

8

The Virgins on Sexuality and Virginity

In all the stories in the Escorial manuscript, women chose to follow a spiritual life. They wanted to free themselves from worldly consider-ations so that they could seek God, a goal that was consistent with orthodox Christian principles and aspirations. However, as we have seen, the ways they chose to lead their new religious lives departed dramatically from the rules for celibate women that Church Fathers were establishing. These women rejected the social expectations that bound their sisters, moved about more freely than the Fathers allowed, came to their own conclusions about the application of Scripture to their own conditions, and generally created lives for themselves that transcended gender expectations.

In the fifth century Palladius wrote *The Lausiac History*, which recounted great deeds of ascetic men and women. In this book, he told an anecdote about Melania the Younger that points up in stark contrast the difference between the Fathers' and the virgins' views about how to lead a chaste life. In this incident, Palladius told of a young woman named Alexandra, who immured herself in a tomb. She received the bare necessities of life through a window so small that it kept her from being seen by anyone. One day, Melania visited her and asked her why she had so buried herself. It is not surprising that Melania, who loved to travel, would ask this in some amazement. Alexandra told her story: "A man was distracted in mind because of me, and rather than scandalize a soul made in the image of God, I betook myself alive to a tomb, lest I seem to cause him suffering or reject him." Melania continued the dialogue through the small window, asking how Alexandra persevered in such a lonely, restricted life. Alexandra answered: "From early dawn to the ninth hour I pray from hour to hour while spinning flax. The rest of the time I go over in my mind the holy patriarchs, prophets, apostles and martyrs. Then I eat my crusts and wait patiently the other hours for my end with good hope."[1] Melania may have been awed by Alexandra's piety and asceticism, but she did not choose to entomb herself. On the contrary, she wandered off to see other interesting sights.

All the Fathers would have approved of Alexandra's chosen way of life. The early Fathers feared sex, located sexuality in women and secluded women to save themselves from temptation. Alexandra sealed herself away from the world so that she would never again tempt a man into desire. It was in this spirit that Tertullian urged women to veil themselves so that no man would be tempted by looking at them. Augustine feared passion, which he equated with pride. He would have approved of Alexandra's humble acceptance of her role as a woman, spinning and praying in quiet seclusion. Melania, however, walked away, choosing neither to hide nor to spin. There is clearly an alternative view of chaste women's roles that contradicted the position of the Fathers. This view was held by Ecdicia in opposition to her husband and Augustine; it was held by all the women whose lives I have told here in opposition to the orders of Jerome and others, and it was probably held by many of the men and women who read and copied the Lives.

The women's alternative view of the best life for chaste women did not exist in a philosophical vacuum. Just as the Fathers' view of sexuality shaped their rules for women, the women had a different view of sexuality upon which they founded their lives and their perceptions of virginity and chastity. It is to this alternative view of sexuality that I will now turn.

First of all, there is no evidence in the Lives to suggest that these women found sex intrinsically evil, sinful or disgusting. They did not repudiate sexuality, because it was too intimately related to reproduction, which they accepted as easily as they accepted their own bodies. Helia's most exuberant praises took the form of reproduction images: "Happy childbirth for the men, the women, the old who are made fecund. ..."[2] There was not the slightest sense of rejection of the carnal in Helia's enthusiastic prayer.

Perhaps an even more vivid praise of reproduction and, in turn, of the sexuality that produced it may be found in the Life of Melania. Melania heard of a woman whose child had died in the womb and was not delivered. Melania arrived, accompanied by her virgins, as a surgeon was cutting out the child in an attempt to save the mother. Melania intervened and tied her belt around the tormented woman's waist. The fetus was delivered and the woman saved. Within this tale is an implied rejection of the surgeon's attempts to deal with the situation, and the grim details of the surgery immediately bring the reader to compassion for the dead child and its distressed mother. The standard solution practiced by the male physician was not only grisly, but was shown to be inadequate when compared to Melania's alternative, miraculous solution. Melania did not just let this anecdote speak for itself. She counteracted the fear and disgust generated by the description of the surgeon's actions by saying that reproduction could not be filthy because God had created it. Only sin was abominable. Furthermore, no bodily part that God had created could be filthy, because through it were born the patriarchs, prophets, apostles and other saints.[3] In this powerful passage Melania not only vindicated reproduction and childbirth, but also accepted and even blessed women's vaginas, which Tertullian had identified as the "Gateway of the Devil."

When the Fathers rejected the physicality that meant sexuality, they also feared and renounced the senses that might lead them to the physical. Since the women did not fear their own bodies, neither did they fear the senses. There is no warning in the Lives to avoid seeing, touching, tasting, smelling or hearing. On the contrary, there were moments in which women acknowledged the senses as a positive good. The sight of Pelagia inspired Bishop Nonnus to greater spirituality, not to sin. Thus, contrary to Tertullian's warnings, sight, even the sight of a beautiful woman, was accepted and, moreover, dignified. In her pilgrimage through the Holy Land, Egeria seemed to see no inconsistency between holiness and traveling in some comfort. Constantina best articulated the theoretical position underlying this acceptance of the sensual: "We need to seek how to please God in our bodily members [as well as spiritually]"; she then proceeded to list all the senses and describe eloquently the beauty they all experience, from the sweetness of tastes to the softness of touch. Instead of rejecting these experiences she said, echoing Melania, that God made the body, so all these experiences must be good. It is only for us not to misuse them.[4]

Patristic fear of sensuality caused the Fathers to urge women to close themselves off from the world; to live like Alexandra, walled away from all sensual experiences. Since the women in the Lives did not express such a fear and revulsion of the physical, neither did they adhere to the predominant patristic metaphor for the chaste life, that of being "closed" to the world. In fact, the Lives are pervaded with images of being "open." Constantina's first prayer for Gallicanus's young daughters was that God " ... open the ears of the virgins. Open the ears of their hearts for my words."[5] Even the Fathers did not object to ears being open for educational purposes; that was the only sense they permitted women to keep "open." However, Constantina continued her prayer: "Open their doors so my words can infuse them with virtue."[6] Constantina's choice of metaphor is a telling one, precisely because it seems forced and redundant after the more logical plea that their ears be open and receptive. In patristic works, the image of "door" had a strong sexual connotation, referring to women's genitals. The policy of enclosure derived in large part from the concept that women should keep their closed doors behind closed doors. Constantina's use of the word in an open context argues both for an acceptance of womanhood and for a rejection of enclosure as a principle.

As we have seen from the narratives, most of these women rejected the principle of enclosure. They rejected it for themselves as individuals, but also for spirituality in general. In the Life of Mary of Egypt, the hagiographer made a point of saying that Zosimas "left the doors that had enclosed him for so long."[7] Zosimas had to leave his monastery in order to achieve the higher spirituality that he discovered in the desert in the person of Mary. Moving about was an accepted value of the ascetic world. In addition, however, it would seem that these women rejected the principle of enclosure not only because it constrained their freedom but also because it did not express a metaphoric reality for them. Women's bodies did not need to be closed to the world for them to experience a spiritual life.

In the miracles of Melania, the metaphor of openness is brought into vivid focus. The hagiographer says that he is going to relate only a few of the many miracles Melania performed; in fact, he relates only three. In the first, a woman was "gripped by an evil demon. Her mouth and lips were closed for many days, so that she could neither talk nor eat. She was in danger of starvation." Melania cured the woman and opened her mouth. In fact, the woman held by a demon was the logical conclusion of patristic requirements for silence and fasting. Melania opened her mouth, freeing her from those requirements, replacing the metaphor of closure with one of openness. In the second miracle, the hagiographer merely says: "Another woman who had suffered from the same disease was cured by Melania."[8] It is significant that she did not cure men suffering from lockjaw; this was a metaphor for the constraints placed on women. Melania's third miracle I have already discussed: in it she opened a woman's womb so that her dead child might be born. All her miracles speak to the principle of openness instead of enclosure, and in them she rejected the patristic view of women and of sexuality.

All these positive images of women's sexuality and sensuality leave us with a paradox. These women vigorously and certainly rejected a sexual life and embraced an ascetic one that involved a renunciation even of sensual comforts, not to mention pleasures. Yet they did not reject sexuality as intrinsically evil, nor did they fear their own sensuality. However, sexuality could not have been unambiguously positive, or these women would not have renounced it so powerfully. What sexuality brought to these women was a loss of liberty. Sex might have been good in the abstract, but when a woman had intercourse she bound herself to concerns of the world and to a pre-set relationship with her partner. As the Fathers repeatedly noted, wives were too busy with domestic concerns to be able to give themselves over to spiritual matters, and all these women were passionately committed to a spiritual life.

But it is important to remember that it was not just a spiritual life they sought. If it were, they could have followed the spiritual path for women as outlined by the Fathers: they could have become like Alexandra, buried in feminine obedience. Instead, they chose to be free to follow their own spiritual paths. Their choices revealed a large diversity – from Egeria's pilgrimages to Melania's changes from stability to movement; from Mary of Egypt's retreat to the desert to Castissima's quiet retreat to a monastery. What marked all of them was that each woman chose her own way, despite all pressure. By renouncing the sexual tie, each woman claimed her personal sovereignty. However, all these women were able to renounce sexual intercourse without renouncing the sexuality of their own bodies. The Fathers were never able to do that.

In the Lives, when the women did express an aversion to sexuality it was a sexuality that resided in the male and, more importantly, it was a male sexuality that would entrap the woman. Constantina calls Gallicanus's lust "diabolical passion,"[9] but it was "diabolical" because it might give him the right to decide her destiny – that is, she might be forced to marry him. The same sentiment pervaded Castissima's fear that her father would acquiesce in her suitor's lust, and her life would no longer be her own. These fears express their view of sex as bondage, tying them to social responsibilities.

Now this might sound as if these women were angry at men and looking for a way to remove them from their lives. However, it is not as simple as that. The problem was not simply that men were oppressing women. These women saw men's sexual desire as oppressing both men and women, because it forced them into a relationship bound by social expectations. In the Lives, once women had clearly established their right to be chaste, they had very close and friendly relationships with men. Melania's husband, Pinian, was portrayed almost as a villain in the beginning of the Life while he was urging his wife to continue their sexual relationship. Once they had both taken vows of chastity, however, they traveled together and his role changed from villain to friend. I admit that this perception is from Melania's point of view; we have no way of knowing how Pinian felt about the altered relationship. But the women in the Lives repeatedly expressed pleasure in close, chaste relationships with men. Castissima and her mentor Agapius were very fond of each other; Mary of Egypt's and Zosimas's lives were bound together in chastity. The relationships between Pelagia and Nonnus, and even Egeria and her many escorts, all reveal that women were not taking vows of chastity to avoid men. They wanted to establish a new relationship with men, one based on chastity, not on sexual intercourse, and this goal reflected their desire to establish new ways of life for themselves.

The women in the stories under discussion were not unique in the early centuries of Christianity in their desire and capacity to establish new relationships with men based on celibacy. Rosemary Radar has detailed a whole series of such male–female friendships during these centuries and in fact sees a paradigm shift in the relationships between men and women, made possible by the celibacy of the early Christian communities.[10] She argues convincingly that " ... celibacy thus became a means by which a less restrictive, more egalitarian type of relationship was able to exist between men and women."[11] One can see evidence for this new kind of relationship in many sources from the early Middle Ages – letters between men and women, to men and women cohabiting in chaste marriages, or even in double monasteries – and what made these relationships possible during that time was the vow of chastity that freed men and women from the roles which governed their relationship.[12] To be realistic, we must note that this ideal friendship based on a mutual renunciation of sex did not always work peaceably. One of the failures was the one with which I began this book: Ecdicia and her husband did not suddenly become close when they renounced their sexual relations. They disagreed on exactly how much freedom Ecdicia had earned by her sexual renunciation. New paradigms are not simple to implement. However, the new possibilities for male–female relationships bear testimony to the fact that these women were not rejecting men. What they were rejecting was the limitation of choice that came with entering into a sexual relationship with men.

This view of sexuality that accepts sex itself as good, and rejects it only because it binds people to the world and its expectations, opens an interesting possibility: that sexuality can be accepted once the constraining nature of the relationship is abandoned. But that option would not have been available to most of the women of the late Roman Empire. They could be free to make their own choices and pursue their spirituality in their own way only by renouncing sexual intercourse.

The way the women's sexual renunciation was portrayed in the narratives is quite different from comparable descriptions in patristic works. The Fathers, from Jerome to Augustine, described their sexual urge as a serious obstacle to their spiritual growth. They were plagued with doubts, dreams and desires. Perhaps one of the most obvious contrasts between the Fathers and the virgins is between Jerome and Mary of Egypt. Both went into the desert to seek ascetic spirituality. Jerome was beset by dreams of women; Mary dreamed of food and drink.[13] Notwithstanding prevailing medieval wisdom that women were insatiable sexually, no sexual temptations seem to have troubled the women in these saints' lives. It is important to recognize, however, that these women do not represent a random sample of medieval women. Just because their sexual renunciation did not seem to present a hardship does not mean that would have been true for all women. In fact, the Life of Melania alludes to other women burdened by their sexuality. Melania frequently questioned the virgins living in her community about their thoughts to be sure that they were not having sexual fantasies.[14]

In general, however, the women did not feel, as the Fathers did, that one had to practice rigorous asceticism in order to conquer lust. The reader will recall that Jerome thought the only way to conquer lust was by rigorous fasting. So strongly did he believe this that he equated fasting with chastity. None of the virgins made such an equation. While most of them fasted, they fasted as a proof of their accomplished spirituality, not as a prerequisite for it. Melania said: "Of all the virtues, fasting is the least. ...." and she left the choice to fast to each individual's personal discretion.[15] In the Life of Castissima, too, the hagiographer reduced the importance of fasting by saying that in the monastery, each monk "keeps the fast as he wishes. ...."[16] So the women did not feel that their bodies needed to be so rigorously tamed as the Fathers did. This view is consistent with the women's general acceptance of their bodies and their comfort with their own sexuality. Renouncing sex did not represent a battle.

This is not to say that these women's commitment to the ascetic life came easily. They may not have been troubled by dreams of renounced intercourse, but they were tempted by recollections of lost status. When the Devil appeared to Pelagia, he did not try to tempt her with images of the sexual experiences from her nights as a prostitute. Instead, he reminded her of the silver, gold and jewels that would no longer be hers. To put her devil behind her, Pelagia immediately gave away all her wealth.[17] Melania, too, said that the hardest part of the ascetic life was not struggling against the flesh, but getting rid of her fortune.[18] She had a practical problem giving up her wealth simply because she had so much of it, but the problem goes deeper. The wealth, the jewels, and indeed the clothing that was of such concern to all the women represented their status or identity in the world.

Women in the classical world belonged primarily to the private sphere of their homes. This was dramatically true in the Greek world, where women were virtually not permitted to go outdoors. Roman women emancipated themselves beyond that, and could move about in the world. Yet as Simone de Beauvoir noted, they were emancipated, but with no real place in the world: "She was free – but for nothing."[19] Their only recognition in the public sphere derived from their family status, as marked by the clothing they wore. The classic and perhaps most vivid example of this is Livy's account of the Roman women's demand that the Oppian Law, a sumptuary law, be repealed so that women could resume wearing their ornaments, fancy dress, and purple stripes on their togas.[20] This incident has been used to describe women's lack of political acumen, but the ability to wear signs of one's status in public was a political statement for women. They were seeking the public recognition that was always given so reluctantly. Lucius Valerius, who argued in favor of the women's petition, perceptively recognized their situation. He said: "No offices, no priesthoods, no triumphs, no decorations, no gifts, no spoils of war can come to them; elegance of appearance, adornment, apparel – these are the woman's badges of honour. . . ."[21]

The reality that women were defined in public largely by what they wore was expressed also on a daily basis. Prostitutes had to acknowledge their profession by a particular article of clothing;[22] women of senatorial families could remove their head veils;[23] and young girls expressed their family's status by wearing clothing with embroidery.[24] Men, too, of course, were defined in part by the clothing they wore,[25] but men had other measures of public definition – their jobs, for example. This is probably why in the saints' lives of men, clothing does not come up as such a significant subject. For men, clothing simply followed the public position; for women, clothing was the public position. When the women in this book had dreams and were tempted by the wealth and clothing they were giving up, they were in fact fearing loss of definition in the public sphere.

All the women under discussion were women of wealth and status, either derived from their families (Castissima or Melania) or from their own efforts (the successful prostitutes, Pelagia and Mary of Egypt). When they renounced their previous lives to embrace an ascetic one, they had to give up the thing which had given them most of their identity in their previous roles: their distinctive clothing. However, although they changed their ways of life, they did not change all their old patterns and concerns. This is why, when they converted to an ascetic life, they often continued to mark their status by their clothing, their new ascetic clothing. We have seen how the significant points of Melania's life were marked by changes in her clothing. This continued throughout the narrative to her death, when she was buried in garments "worthy of her holiness."[26] She had transcended all worldly desires except to be publicly recognized for what she had accomplished.

Most of the other women in these narratives shared Melania's desire to use clothing to mark their freedom from men, and from traditional women's roles. This was true of Ecdicia, who wore widow's clothing to demonstrate her new chastity even though her husband was still alive. It was certainly true of Pelagia and Castissima, who wore men's clothing to demonstrate their renunciation. It was even true of Mary of Egypt, who, after her clothing had rotted away in the desert, said she was dressed in the word of God.[27] The only Life in which the clothing theme does not emerge as a significant one is the Life of Constantina. It seems likely that Constantina, as the daughter of the Emperor, had so much public status that she did not need to be so careful to express it by her clothing. Within the Life, her status was defined by the repeated use of the title "Augusta" to acknowledge her as the Emperor's daughter. The virgins, then, in their struggle to free themselves from the expected roles that bound them in society, continued to want public recognition for themselves. A private renunciation was not enough. This is probably why they were tempted not by dreams of sex, but by dreams of the wealth and clothing that had traditionally provided their public definition.

The women we have been looking at were successful in their desire to shape a new way of life for themselves. They built lives of chastity based not on a patristic vision but on their own view of themselves and their needs. This view reveals not only a different perception of sexuality from that of the Fathers, but also a different perception of virginity and chastity. One of the most striking differences is that the narratives of the Lives do not distinguish in any significant way between whether the women were virgins, like Castissima and Constantina, or chaste wives, like Melania, or even ex-prostitutes, like Pelagia and Mary of Egypt. Because of their vows of chastity, all these women are portrayed with the same degree of dignity and sanctity, and all receive the same privileges. This suggests that, unlike the Fathers, they saw women's sexuality as a state, a choice, not a permanent, magical condition. When a woman was engaged in a sexual relationship, she lost personal sovereignty; when she renounced intercourse, she regained her freedom and status. This is a far cry from Jerome's view that the integrity of virginity is such a supernatural state that even God could not restore a fallen virgin. Jerome and the other Fathers saw women as bound by their bodies, slaves to their own carnality, with their destiny determined by the state of their hymen. The women in this book were much more at ease with their own bodies, with their sexuality, and felt their destiny should be determined by choice.

As we have seen throughout the Lives, the prevailing image of chastity for women was freedom. With the initial choice of freedom from sexual intercourse, other freedoms seem to come as well. While Melania was living with Pinian as a wife, she obeyed him. As soon as they took vows of chastity she became the leader in the relationship, telling Pinian what to wear and where to live. The lesson can be seen more subtly in the other Lives. For example, when Mary of Egypt was still a prostitute, she could not enter the church; she was magically prevented

from doing so. As soon as she had taken a vow of chastity she was free
to enter; the constraints were lifted. By such associations of freedom
with chastity, the women departed radically from the Fathers' associations of chastity with restraint and humility.

The narratives do accept some of the patristic images for chastity, but
only those that enhance the dignity of the women involved. The careful
selection of patristic work was shown most clearly in the Life of Helia,
but the rest of the Lives reveal the same preference for certain types of
images. The two images most favored in the Lives are the bride of Christ
image and the associations of chastity with fertility. The attraction to the
bride of Christ image is fairly obvious. By being Christ's bride, a
woman's status in the world with regard to everyone else was elevated,
and such a status was often convenient. For example, Constantina
argued that by remaining true to their husband, Christ, Gallicanus's
daughters would be "*univira*," women who remained true to only one
husband. Such women were highly respected in the Empire, so the bride
of Christ metaphor was used to bring status in a way familiar to the
Romans.

The second popular image, that of fertility, fits well with the women's
view of sexuality in which their bodies and their reproductive function
are not disdained. Again, the narrative of the Life of Helia is rich with
such images, but the images are not limited to that Life. The Life of
Constantina, for example, contains a wonderful praise of St Agnes in
which Agnes's care is described as rich and fertile, and she is portrayed
as "suckling" those under her protection.[28] Even in smaller incidences
fertility images abound. When Castissima spoke to a monk, "her heart
was irrigated by his words."[29] The examples could be multiplied, but the
significant point is to recognize the degree to which a cohesive body of
thought is expressed in these narratives. The woman's ascetic view
presents a vision of women that does not reject their bodies or their
sexuality, and this acceptance is brought to its vision of chastity.

All these women renounced lives that included sexual intercourse in
favor of a better life, a life that Constantina called the "highest good."[30]
This way of life was first and foremost spiritual. One would not want to
lose sight of the fact that these women – indeed, all the ascetics – were
seeking God. Yet the second fundamental fact of the ascetic life was that
it was individual. Each woman felt that she could best find God in her
own way, and the freedom implicit in this value extended to other
aspects of her life. Thus, when we look at the specific values that under-
lie these ways of life, we can discern significant differences from the
patristic dictates that were designed to guide women to chaste
spirituality.

After freedom of choice, one of the values that emerges as important in a chaste way of life for many of these ascetic women was a close-knit, supportive community. With some exceptions (Mary of Egypt, Castissima and Pelagia) the women valued their ties with a community of women like themselves. Constantina surrounded herself with 120 women – living with her, as the hagiographer said, "in a kind of family."[31] Egeria's letter to her community is full of affection and caring. Melania, after a period of ascetic solitude, surrounded herself with a community of virgins, but she also showed the importance of female companionship in her friendship with the Empress Eudocia. The hagiographer said of the two women that they "were scarcely able to be separated from one another, for they were strongly bonded together in spiritual love."[32] There is nothing in the Lives to indicate that by giving up sexual intercourse these women gave up close, nurturing relationships. Quite the contrary, for Constantina says: "When you have virginity whole, you always have love."[33]

The Fathers were most concerned that women within communities be strictly bound by obedience to their superiors, so that spiritual women's roles would parallel the expected roles of secular women. The narratives of the Lives of the ascetic women repeatedly show that obedience was not a high value. Most of them did not even discuss the question of obedience, they just did as they pleased. The Life of Melania, however, presents a more detailed consideration of the place and nature of obedience in these ascetic communities.

When Melania organized her community of women, she did not assume the role of Mother Superior to the house; she appointed someone else. Gerontius, the hagiographer, attributed this to her "excess of humility,"[34] but it was a very strange form of humility, for she never particularly acceded to the Mother Superior's authority. For example, whenever Melania decided the Mother Superior was too rigid in her treatment of the women, she would care for her "weaker sisters" by leaving extra items in their cells in violation of the Mother Superior's wishes.[35] Gerontius relates this incident to show Melania's "boundless compassion," but in fact it is equally revealing of her independence of all authority.

Melania's views on authority are further shown by her instructions to her virgins on the virtue of obedience. At first glance, this seems to be exactly the sort of exhortation that Jerome or Augustine might make to nuns. Upon closer consideration, however, one can see that Melania was not talking about a strictly hierarchical principle. She described obedience as a mutual respect in which, for example, "even worldly rulers submit and obey each other." Therefore, the lesson she drew was that "all ought to be obedient to each other."[36] The communal life described by Melania was not a difficult one, the requirements for obedience were not exacting, and the community was to be close and nurturing. Further-more, in the general spirit of personal sovereignty and choice that pervades these Lives, the day-to-day life the women followed within the community was not strictly prescribed, and not as restricted as that demanded by the Fathers.

The key to the spiritual life as articulated in these Lives is education. The spirituality women sought was intimately tied to their ability to read, write and understand the sacred texts and other Christian works. In the Life of Constantina, the conversion of Gallicanus's daughters was precipitated by, and intimately associated with their education, to the degree that when Constantina told Gallicanus about the conversion, she described how "learned they have become."[37] Castissima was also known for an early education that enhanced her spiritual progress. In her youth, she was renowned not only for goodness or virtue (although those qualities were present) but was also famous throughout the city for her "wisdom and love of learning."[38] Egeria, too, reveals a strong pre-occupation with study, for in her travels to the Holy Land she collected copies of letters to enhance some works that the community held in Spain. In her letter to the virgins at home, she described these acquisi-tions with pride and said she could not wait to share them with her sisters.[39] The Life of Melania also stresses the theme of the importance of education, but characteristically it yokes this theme with that of independence. Gerontius said that Melania "decided for herself how much she ought to write every day, how much she should read in the canonical works and how much in the collections of sermons."[40]

The early Fathers, like Jerome, also stressed education in the service of spiritual growth. Augustine emphasized it less, for it might lead to pride. He preferred to see women involved in more traditional female occupations like spinning, so that they might remain humble. The Lives in this ascetic tradition departed from the views of even the early Fathers, however, when they addressed what women were to do with such learning. The Fathers believed that women should be silent, keep-ing their learning to themselves and being living examples of closed, mute chastity. In the ascetic tradition, however, these educated holy women were not silent. They taught, preached and explicated Scripture. Zosimas urged Mary of Egypt to speak to instruct him;[41] Constantina explicated Scripture;[42] Melania was a "divinely inspired teacher" who "did not stop discussing theology from dawn to dusk."[43]

These differences between the Fathers and the virgins in their percep-tions of how women should lead a chaste life derive from their differing views of sexuality and womanhood. The women in the ascetic tradition were not afraid of their sexuality, nor were they ashamed of their gender. Therefore there was no reason to restrict their liberty once they had removed themselves from the commitments of sexual intercourse. They pursued their own spiritual paths in a society that did not have a clearly defined place for them. I have been discussing this alternative view of sexuality and virginity from the examples of a handful of women. It remains to consider the impact of narratives like these that articulated this different viewpoint.

During the early centuries of Christianity, this ascetic perspective was a body of thought that was one among many possible directions Western Christianity could have selected. This view was not insignificant in its contemporary impact. Palladius said that his book was "written also to commemorate women far advanced in years and illustrious God-inspired mothers who have performed feats of virtuous asceticism in strong and perfect intention, as exemplars. ..."[44] These women, like the women commemorated in the Escorial manuscript, were influential in articulating not only an ascetic way of life but also an ascetic body of thought that offered an independence attractive to many women. Such women adopted a chaste life that permitted the kinds of freedoms Melania and others were enjoying. They spread the ideal from the East all over the Empire. Ambrose gave credit where credit was due, and said that he was only describing the virgin life; it was the women who had initiated it.[45] As Jo Ann McNamara forcefully stated:

> These women conceived and carried out a revolution of vast proportions. They forced the social structure of antiquity to incorporate the celibate woman in a secure and even superior stratum. Some of the men who commented on the process were hostile and fearful of the new order developing in their midst.[46]

Among the men who were concerned about the impact of this option for a Christian life were the Fathers who legislated so prolifically about how virgins should live. The volume of writings on the subject by Jerome, Ambrose, Augustine and others suggests that they were trying to control a popular movement. That is perhaps most clear in the writings of Tertullian, who, writing in the late second century, was closest to the beginnings of the ascetic movement. In his tract "On the Veiling of Virgins," he specifically says that he is against virgins claiming freedoms that married women do not have – freedoms such as speaking in church, teaching, baptizing and holding ecclesiastical offices.[47] The freedoms he is trying to restrict are exactly the kinds of liberties ascetic women were claiming. Tertullian wanted to limit choice on many levels – for example, he said, regarding virgins veiling their heads: "[Up until recently] the matter had been left to choice, for each virgin to veil herself or expose herself as she might have chosen. ..."[48] Tertullian was

afraid of the social ramifications of giving some women so much freedom, so he was vehement in his desire to restrict it.

By the fourth and fifth centuries, the Church was beginning to
become more strictly organized. Homogeneity of belief and obedience
to hierarchy began to be enforced. Under the weight of patristic
pressure, fewer and fewer women were able to live an ascetic life that
valued freedom of choice as part of its central theme, and accepted
women's sexuality as no hindrance to sanctity. Yet in spite of the
Fathers' influence, this body of ideas was not lost.

Throughout the Middle Ages, saints' lives like these were widely
copied and translated from Latin into vernacular languages. As they
were copied century after century, copyists were affirming that the
values and ideas embodied in the Lives were worth preserving, even if
they did not adhere to the strict dictates of the orthodox Church. Not
only were Lives like these copied, but they were read and used as exemplars. The Escorial manuscript that I have been using for a sample of
this type of narrative was a *Codex Regularum*. This means it was a
collection of monastic writings that served as a rule for monks and nuns
to follow in their lives. The inclusion of the saints' lives in such a codex
ensured that they would be read seriously. It appears that the Church
was not as successful as it would have liked to be at eliminating the
variety of ideas that originated in the freer, early centuries of Christianity. Of course, most of the women who read and copied these narratives
could not appreciably change their own lives, but perhaps they took
pleasure in the examples of these women, and perhaps they took
comfort in the underlying view of sexuality and womanhood that was in
such contrast to the patristic view they were living. In any case, the ideas
were preserved by men and women who saved the ascetic vision,
perhaps until such time as diversity of opinion would be accepted in the
West.

The fact that this ascetic view of women was saved for over a millen-
nium in itself warrants its presentation here. Too many people worked
to preserve it for it to be lost. Yet after all these centuries, and all these
pages, it may not be inappropriate to consider what these women's lives
have to say to us. First and most importantly, the recognition of these
ideas lets us reclaim a portion of our past. People who are exploring the
ideas that have historically bound women into predetermined roles can
look to a long-standing alternative body of thought that gave women
both dignity and independence, and this body of thought is as venerable
as some of the most restrictive ideas. Furthermore, people who are
trying to explore new ways of looking at sexuality that are not bound to
the negative view articulated by the Church Fathers need not think they
are working in a historical vacuum. Throughout the Christian era there

have been men and women who have seen sexuality and the relationship between men and women in terms different from the patristic view that has dominated Western thought. Those ideas, too, are our intellectual history. In this alternative ascetic view that can still speak to us, the problem with sexuality lies not within our bodies but within social patterns that see biology as destiny, sexual intercourse as determining social intercourse, and a social intercourse that arbitrarily restricts freedom of choice.

The Manuscript Tradition

The Lives I have discussed were all drawn from one Visigothic codex, but they had a longer history and a wider distribution than one manuscript. Here I will give a brief summary of the probable compilation of this particular manuscript, which will also indicate the broad movement of texts and ideas throughout the early medieval Mediterranean world.

In the fifth century, three of the Lives were composed in the Eastern Mediterranean: the Lives of Melania, Pelagia and Euphrosyne (this one became the Life of Castissima in Iberia). These Lives were probably written in Greek, and were copied and treasured in the East as offering models of holiness. Also, early in the fifth century, the Life of Helia was written in Spain. However, the reader will recall that even the locally composed Life of Helia was based on ideas in the writings of Jerome sent to Iberia from the Holy Land, so this Life was also heavily indebted to the Eastern ascetic sensibility.

In the sixth century the Life of Constantina was compiled in Latin, probably in Italy. In this century there were many interactions between the East and the Iberian peninsula. For example, one holy man from the East, Donatus, traveled through North Africa and crossed into Spain. In the seventh century, Ildephonse of Toledo included Donatus in his list of illustrious men, noting his contribution to Iberian monasticism. Ildephonse said Donatus brought Greek saints' lives into Spain along with his Eastern monastic ideals.[1] I cannot prove that the collection brought by Donatus included the popular Greek Lives of Melania, Pelagia, and Euphrosyne/Castissima, but it is possible. Certainly, if Donatus himself did not bring these Lives to the Iberian peninsula, someone like him did.

Once in Spain, the Lives were translated from Greek to Latin. We know that there was such translation going on in Iberia in the sixth century. Paschasius of Dumium translated the *Sayings of the Desert*

129

Fathers from Greek to Latin, and it is possible that he or one of his students translated the Greek Lives.

Antolín, an eminent scholar of Visigothic manuscripts, believed that Paschasius was involved with at least one of the Lives, that of St Helia. The Life of St Helia seems to have two introductions, and Antolín believes that the first one was written by Paschasius because the language was similar to his other writings.[2] If this is true, then the Life composed by Theodora in the fifth century passed through Paschasius's hands in the sixth century. By the sixth century, then, it is likely that five of the seven Lives in the Escorial manuscript were circulating in Iberia.

In the early seventh century, the Life of Mary of Egypt was written in Greek, probably by Sophronius, patriarch of Jerusalem. This was a popular Life that circulated widely, and was translated into Latin.[3] I cannot identify exactly when the *Vita* entered Spain, but it was early enough for the version in the codex discussed here to be considered one of the significant ones in the early manuscript tradition.[4]

Also in the seventh century, Valerius of Bierzo wrote his praise of the fourth-century virgin Etheria (Egeria), who traveled to the Holy Land and wrote letters to her Iberian spiritual sisters. This panegyric also was eventually included in the Escorial manuscript.

Thus by the eighth century all the Lives that would be collected into the Escorial codex were available in the Iberian peninsula. These Lives must have been saved by monks and nuns fleeing north from the eighth-century Moslem invasions that brought down the Visigothic kingdom. The Christian kingdoms survived in the hilly north-west provinces of Iberia, and from there Christians waged the slow seven-hundred-year reconquest of the peninsula. Christianity and the precious Christian texts were preserved behind monastery walls during the obscure century and a half that followed the Moslem invasion. One Iberian manuscript surviving from the eighth century contains portions of the Life of Melania, but it is jumbled with the life of Saint Pelagia.[5] This manuscript is now in Chartres, but it bears an imperfect witness to the Iberian preservation of two of these saints' lives through the difficult century of invasion in Spain.

From the late ninth or early tenth century, we can again pick up a more direct transmission leading to the compilation of the codex of women's saints' lives. In about AD 912, Leodegúndia, a nun in the monastery of Bobatelle, copied (and signed) a manuscript containing religious writings. The monastery was located in north-west Iberia, probably affiliated with the famous monastery of Samos.[6] This manuscript is preserved in the Escorial as number a I 13.[7] In this Appendix, I shall designate this manuscript as **a**. There is a controversy about the dating of this manuscript, because Leodegúndia indicated the date 912 in the reign of King Alfonso,[8] but King Alfonso was not ruling in 912. Thus the manuscript may date from as early as 812 (in the reign of Alfonso II)[9] to as late as 927 (in the reign of Alfonso III).[10]

Leodegúndia collected texts of interest to her monastic audience. She included monastic rules of Saints Benedict, Isidore, Leander and Fructuosus, letters from Jerome (to Eustochium, Furia, and others) and the Lives of Constantina and Melania. These are the oldest complete surviving Latin versions of these Lives. Leodegúndia's collection shows the transmission of the full ascetic tradition, including patristic works and the works that expressed the ascetic women's ideals.

A short time later, still early in the tenth century, another scribe, perhaps another nun in Leodegúndia's monastery, copied the Lives of Constantina and Melania from the a manuscript and combined them with other saints' lives to form the collection I have studied in this book. This manuscript has been lost, but by comparing the Lives of Constantina and Melania in Leodegúndia's a manuscript with the later surviving redactions it is possible to assume the existence of this hypothetical compilation with reasonable certainty. I shall designate this lost manuscript as y.

The scribe who compiled the lost y manuscript took some liberties with the a text. This scribe must have seen things in common among the seven Lives she or he was putting together from several different codices. This was not just mindless copying. For example, from the a manuscript the scribe took the Lives of Melania and Constantina, omitting the patristic works. He or she then added other women's saints' lives to the codex, creating a collection of ascetic women saints' lives that was copied by scribes of at least the two surviving codices of the whole collection. These manuscripts are the tenth-century Escorial manuscript number a II 9 (designated here as b) and the eleventh-century manuscript number 2178 in the Bibliothèque National de Paris, nouveau acquisition (designated here as c). Beyond selecting works from a, the y scribe made a number of small changes in the texts. For example, in the Melania text, fifty-four minor word substitutions were made by the y scribe. Some were small changes – for example, the scribe replaced "*que*" with "*cum*"[11] or "*igitur*" with "*ergo*".[12] Other word substitutions represent a bit more of a change:

a   "*esse sine perturbatione*"

b   "*esse sine tristitia*"

c   "*esse sine tristitia*"[13]

These changes made by the y scribe did not appreciably alter the meaning of the text, but since they were faithfully copied by the **b** and **c** scribes, they help to demonstrate that **b** and **c** were not directly copied from **a**, thus corroborating the existence of the lost **y** manuscript.

The **y** scribe also added forty-five marginal notes to **a**'s original twenty-one. Most of these notes were short summaries of the material in the text that would permit a reader to find a particular passage more quickly. It seems that the **y** scribe wanted to make the collection accessible and useful.

In 954, a notary named John copied the collection of saints' lives from the **y** codex to form the **b** manuscript.[14] Depending on the date we accept for **a**, it would have been anywhere from twenty-seven to a hundred and forty-two years between the compilation of the **y** manuscript and John's copying of it. Accepting Leodegúndia's date of 912 would have allowed forty-two years. Since all three manuscripts were copied in northern Spain, any of the dates allows for this sequence of copying.

John did not take as many liberties with the text as did the scribe of **y**, probably in part because he copied the whole collection of saints' lives that had been amassed by **y**. John added ten words and phrases to **y** and dropped ten words and phrases. One example of such an addition may be seen by the following comparisons:

a, c *"Illius beatissime ualeamus. Igitur Ipsa*
beatissima ..."

b   *"Illius beatissime valeamus pinnianus melaniae.*
Igitur ipsa beatissima ..."[15]

Most of the words omitted by John were prepositions he must have found superfluous; for example:

a, c *"Quum igitur in his constituta ..."*

b   *"Quum igitur his constituta ..."*[16]

These changes are minor; they serve to indicate that John the Notary made small idiosyncratic changes to the text at hand. What is important about these changes is that the copyist of **c** did not incorporate any of them, but in fact returned to the language of **a**, once again showing the probability of a lost intermediary manuscript.

In addition to the saints' lives drawn from **y**, the **b** manuscript contains St Ildephonse of Toledo's *"De Virginitate Mariae,"* Jerome's works *"Adversus Jovinianus"* and *"Contra Helvidius"* in the beginning of the folio volume, and Saint Braulio's *"Vita St Aemyliani"* at the end.

These works were in a different hand, added by a different scribe, no doubt someone who believed that these writings on the subject of virginity would enhance the lesson of the seven saints' lives. Braulio's "*Vita St Aemyliani*" begins on fol. 133, after the folio that identified John as the scribe, so it is reasonable to assume that John copied the corpus of saints' lives from **y**, and an anonymous scribe added the works in front and at the end of the corpus.

In the middle of the eleventh century, the **c** scribe copied the **y** codex, possibly at the monastery of Silos. This scribe took even fewer liberties with the text than John did of manuscript **b**. He or she added nothing, but omitted nine words and two lines from **y**, seemingly scribal errors.[17]

The **c** scribe kept most of the marginal notes added by **y**, even those omitted by **b**. The improbability of the random occurrence of the exact note in the exact place on two manuscripts is so great that it virtually assures that **c** was copied either from **a** or from an intermediary which contained the note from **a**. Since there are a large number of phrases in common between **b** and **c** that do not exist on **a**, the scribe of **c** could not have copied the manuscript directly from **a**. Therefore, the existence of the lost manuscript **y** seems virtually certain.

This summary gives the direct development of the Iberian manuscript tradition of this codex. However, one should remember that the preservation of the ascetic women's tradition was not limited to the Iberian peninsula. Throughout the Middle Ages all these Lives, except those of Helia and Etheria, spread widely and continued to be copied. For example, there is an eleventh-century copy of the Life of Castissima in the Escorial (manuscript number **b** I 4). The Bollandist Paris Catalogue shows twelfth- and thirteenth-century manuscripts of the Lives of Mary of Egypt and Pelagia. Versions of the Mary of Egypt Life were even translated into the vernacular in the late Middle Ages.[18] The ascetic view of sexuality and womanhood as expressed in these Lives had a long and popular tradition.

Notes

Introduction

1. Augustine, Letter No. 262, in *Saint Augustine: Letters vol. V*, transl. W. Parsons, New York 1956, p. 261.

2. Ibid., p. 264.

3. James A. Brundage, *Law, Sex, and Christian Society in Medieval Europe*, Chicago 1987, pp. 5, 580–81.

4. See D. J. Chitty, *The Desert a City: An Introduction to the Study of Egyptian and Palestinian Monasticism under the Christian Empire*, Oxford 1966, for a discussion of the origins of Eastern ascetic monasticism.

5. For the function of holy people in society, see Peter Brown, "The Rise and Function of the Holy Man in Late Antiquity," *Journal of Roman Studies*, 61, 1971, pp. 80–101.

6. John Bugge, *Virginitas: An Essay in the History of a Medieval Ideal*, The Hague 1975, p. 30.

7. Montague Rhodes James, *The Apocryphal New Testament*, Oxford 1969, p. 420.

8. Ibid., p. 438.

9. Stevan Davies, *The Revolt of the Widows: The Social World of the Apocryphal Acts*, Carbondale, IL 1980, p. 95. See also Ross Kraemer, "The Conversion of Women to Ascetic Forms of Christianity," *Signs* VI, 1980/81, pp. 298–307, for a discussion of the appeal of these Acts to women whose lives were in transition.

10. Davies, p. 103.

11. See Joyce Salisbury, "Fruitful in Singleness," *Journal of Medieval History*, 8, 1982, pp. 97–102.

12. Jo Ann McNamara, *A New Song: Celibate Women in the First Three Christian Centuries*, New York 1983, p. 3. See also R. Reuther and E. McLaughlin, eds, *Women of Spirit: Female Leadership in the Jewish and Christian Traditions*, New York 1979, p. 73, in which they argue that asceticism was a "liberating choice for women."

13. Hippolyte Delehaye, "Les Femmes Stylites," *Analecta Bollandiana* 27, 1908, pp. 391–2.

14. Margot King, *The Desert Mothers: A Survey of the Feminine Anchoretic Tradition*, Saskatoon, SK 1984, pp. 2–3.

15. See Jeffrey Burton Russell, *Prophecy and Order*, New York 1971, for an analysis of the struggle between individualism and hierarchy.

16. See, for example, Philippe Ariès, in *Western Sexuality*, Oxford 1985, p. 37: "The Roman citizen ... must never play a passive role in love, whether homosexual or heterosexual."

17. Isidore of Seville, *Etimologias, vols I & II*, ed. J. Oroz Reta and M. Marcos Casquero, Madrid 1982, xi, 2, 18–19, p. 43.

18. James A. Brundage, "Let Me Count the Ways: Canonists and Theologians Contemplate Coital Positions," *Journal of Medieval History* 10, 1984, p. 87.

19. See, for example, Council of Elvira, canons XIII and XIV, in *Patrologiae Cursus Completus, Series Latina* (hereafter *PL*). 84:303; First Council of Toledo, canon XVI, *PL* 84:331.

20. See Third Council of Toledo, canon IV, *PL* 84:352; Fourth Council of Toledo, canon LI, *PL* 84:442–3. It is perhaps useful to note that the same kind of controlling impulse was going on for male ascetics at the same time.

21. King, pp. 9–16.

22. McNamara, p. 98.

23. Agnes Smith Lewis, *Select Narratives of Holy Women: Syriac Text, Studia Sinaitica X*, London 1900, pp. vi–vii.

24. Ibid., p. vi.

25. This manuscript is Escorial (Esc.) a II 9. An eleventh-century Spanish copy may be found in the Bibliothèque Nationale, Paris, nouveau acquisitions, MS. 2178.

26. Escorial MS. a I 13, fol. 186v.

27. Esc. a II 9, fol. 132v, reveals the name of the scribe and the date of the copy.

PART I
The Fathers

1 The Early Fathers on Sexuality

1. James A. Brundage, *Law, Sex, and Christian Society*, p. 79.

2. S. Laeuchli, *Power and Sexuality: The Emergence of Canon Law at the Synod of Elvira*, Philadelphia 1972, pp. 102–13.

3. Jerome, "To Eustochium," in *Nicene and Post-Nicene Fathers, Second Series*, vol. VI, ed. P. Schaff and H. Wace, New York 1893, p. 23. (Hereinafter cited as *Nicene Fathers*.)

4. Cyprian, "The Dress of Virgins," in *Treatises*, transl. R. J. Deferrari, New York 1958, p. 34.

5. Ibid., p. 35.

6. Ambrose, "Concerning Virgins," in *Nicene Fathers*, vol. X, p. 376; Jerome, "To Eustochium," ibid., vol. VI, p. 31.

7. See Peter Brown, *The Cult of Saints*, Chicago 1981, for a discussion on the growing importance of relics in the early centuries of Christianity.

8. Jerome, "To Eustochium," p. 24.

9. Jerome, "Against Jovinian," in *Nicene Fathers*, vol. VI, p. 359.

10. Jerome, "The Perpetual Virginity of the Blessed Virgin Mary, Against Helvidius," in *Nicene Fathers*, vol. VI, p. 345; Ambrose, *On Virginity*, transl. David Callam, Saskatoon, SK 1980, p. 11.

11. Jerome, "Against Jovinian," p. 356; Ambrose, *On Virginity*, p. 11.

12. Jerome, "Against Jovinian," p. 386.

13. Tertullian, "One Exhortation to Chastity" in *Ante-Nicene Fathers*, vol. IV, Grand Rapids, MI 1951, p. 55.

14. See, for examples, Ambrose, *On Virginity*, p. 9; Jerome, "Perpetual Virginity," p. 345.

15. Tertullian, "To His Wife," in *Ante-Nicene Fathers*, vol. IV, p. 39; Jerome, "Against Jovinian," p. 357.

16. Jerome, "Against Jovinian," p. 374.

17. Tertullian, "On the Apparel of Women," in *Tertullian: Disciplinary, Moral and Ascetical Works*, ed. R.J. Deferrari, New York 1959, p. 134.

18. Cyprian, "The Dress of Virgins," in *Saint Cyprian: Treatises*, transl. R. J. Deferrari, New York 1958, p. 5.

19. Ambrose, "Concerning Virgins," in *Nicene Fathers*, vol. X, p. 371. See also Jerome, "To Eustochium," p. 30, for association of virginity with the angelic life.

20. Jerome, "Against Jovinian," pp. 351, 371.

21. Ambrose, "De Institutione Virginitate," *PL* 16:321.

22. Tertullian, "Exhortation to Chastity," p. 55.

23. Jerome, "To Eustochium," p. 28.

24. Jerome, "To Demetrias," in *Nicene Fathers*, vol. VI, p. 248.

25. Derrick Sherwin Bailey, *Sexual Relation in Christian Thought*, New York 1959, p. 43–4, notes: "In the patristic treatment of sexual and matrimonial topics one feature particularly compels attention – namely a curious and sometimes almost morbid preoccupation with physical sexuality."

26. Ambrose, Letter No. 25, in *Saint Ambrose: Letters*, transl. Sister M. M. Beyenke, New York 1954, p. 132.

27. Jerome, "Against Jovinian," p. 350.

28. Pseudo-Clement, "Two Epistles Concerning Virginity," in *Ante-Nicene Fathers*, vol. III, ed. A. Roberts and J. Donaldson, Grand Rapids 1951, p. 61.

29. Jerome, "To Eustochium," p. 25.

30. Jerome, "To Furia," in *Nicene Fathers*, vol. VI, pp. 105–6.

31. Jerome, "To Eustochium," p. 35.

32. Tertullian, "On the Veiling of Virgins," in *Ante-Nicene Fathers*, vol. IV, p. 37.

33. Cyprian, "The Dress of Virgins," p. 39.

34. Jerome, "To Rusticus," in *Nicene Fathers*, vol. VI, p. 246.

35. Tertullian, "On the Apparel of Women," p. 132.

36. Ambrose, "De Institutione Virginitate," *PL* 16:320.

37. Ambrose, *On Virginity*, p. 17.

38. Ambrose, "Concerning Virgins," p. 369.

39. Ambrose, *On Virginity*, pp. 24–5.

40. Ibid., p. 23.

41. Ibid., p. 17.

42. Ambrose, "De Institutione Virginitate," *PL* 16:337.

43. Jerome, "To Furia," p. 105.

44. Jerome, "To Demetrias," p. 267.

45. Jerome, "To Eustochium," p. 24.

46. Ambrose, Letter No. 86, in *Saint Ambrose: Letters*, p. 481.

47. Ambrose, "Concerning Widows," in *Nicene Fathers*, vol. X, p. 406.

48. Jerome, "To Ageruchia," in *Nicene Fathers*, vol. VI, p. 234. For other similar references, see Jerome, "Against Jovinian," p. 376; Ambrose, "Concerning Widows," p. 391; Tertullian, "To His Wife," p. 43.

49. Jerome, "To Eustochium," p. 25.

50. Jerome, "To Ageruchia," p. 235.

51. Jerome, "To Demetrias," p. 267.

52. Jerome, "To Eustochium," p. 24.

53. Jerome, "To Salvina," in *Nicene Fathers*, vol. VI, p. 166.

54. Jerome, "To Furia," p. 105.

55. Ambrose, Letter No. 57, in *Saint Ambrose: Letters*, p. 314.

56. Jerome, "To Ageruchia," p. 236.

57. Jerome, "To Furia," p. 105.

58. Ambrose, "Concerning Widows," p. 392. For similar statements concerning cooling with age, see Jerome, "To Furia," p. 105; Tertullian, "On the Apparel of Women," p. 141.

59. Jerome, "Against Jovinian," p. 361.

60. Ibid., pp. 371, 376.

61. Isidore of Seville, *Etimologias*, vol. I, ed. J. Oroz Reta and M. Marcos Casquero, Madrid 1982, ix, 7, 30, p. 801.

62. Isidore of Seville, "De Ecclesiasticis Officiis, Lib. II," xx, 6 *PL* 83:811.

63. Ambrose, Letter No. 78, in *Saint Ambrose: Letters*, p. 435.

64. Jerome, "Against Jovinian," p. 374.

65. Jerome, "To Eustochium," p. 26; Isidore, *Etimologias* XI, 1, 98, p. 29.

66. Paul Veyne, "Homosexuality in Ancient Rome," in *Western Sexuality: Practice*

and Precept in Past and Present Times, ed. P. Ariès and A. Béjin, Oxford 1985, p. 29.

67. Isidore, *Etimologias* X, 179, p. 835. Ariès, in *Western Sexuality*, p. 37, also noted that this identification of masturbation with effeminacy was common in the late Empire.

68. Isidore, *Etimologias* X, 179, p. 835.

69. Ambrose, "De Institutione Virginitate," *PL* 16:325.

70. Isidore, *Etimologias* xi, 24, p. 43. V. L. Bullough, *The Subordinate Sex: A History of Attitudes Toward Women*, Urbana 1973, p. 119, saw early Christian suspicions of women as sexual creatures as deriving from a male-centered asceticism. This is true, but I think the male-centered asceticism derived from a dualist view of the world that placed women in the carnal realm.

71. Jerome, "Against Jovinian," p. 367.

72. Ambrose, "De Institutione Virginitate," *PL* 16:326.

73. Tertullian, "On the Apparel of Women," p. 118. See also F. Forrester Church, "Sex and Salvation in Tertullian," *Harvard Theological Review*, 68, April 1975, pp. 83–101, where he discusses Tertullian's misogynist reputation and attempts to understand it in the context of the times.

74. Tertullian, "On the Apparel of Women," p. 117.

75. Jerome, "To Furia," p. 104. See also Ambrose, "Concerning Virgins," p. 385, where he refers to women loosening their hair as an act of seduction.

76. Isidore, *Etimologias* xi, 1, 141, pp. 37–9.

77. Tertullian, "To His Wife," p. 43.

78. Ambrose, Letter No. 59, in *Saint Ambrose: Letters*, p. 361.

79. Tertullian, "On the Veiling of Virgins," p. 37.

80. Jerome, "To Ageruchia," p. 232.

81. Jerome, "Against Jovinian," p. 375.

2 The Early Fathers on Virginity

1. For a general discussion on the value of virginity in the abstract, the best work remains Bugge, *Virginitas*.

2. Jerome, "Commentariorum in epistolam and ephesios libri 3," *PL* 26:533.

3. Ambrose, "Expositio Evangeliis Secundum Lucam," *PL* 15:1844.

4. McNamara, *A New Song*, p. 109.

5. Tertullian, "On the Veiling of Virgins," p. 31.

6. Ibid., pp. 30–31, 34.

7. Ibid., p. 34.

8. Ibid., p. 37.

9. Demetrius Dumm, *The Theological Basis of Virginity According to St Jerome*, Latrobe, PA 1961, p. 32.

10. See, for example, Jerome, "Against Jovinian," p. 347, where he says: "... while we honor marriage we prefer virginity which is the offspring of marriage. Will silver cease to be silver if gold is more precious than silver?"

11. Ambrose, "Concerning Widows," p. 405. See also Jerome, "To Ageruchia," p. 2.

12. Jerome, "To Eustochium," p. 23. Ambrose, too, observes similar disadvantages in "Concerning Virgins," p. 367.

13. Jerome, "To Demetrias," p. 4.

14. Ambrose, "Concerning Virgins," p. 365. Jerome expressed the same comparison in "To Demetrias," p. 3.

15. Jean LaPorte, *The Role of Women in Early Christianity*, New York 1982, p. 64.

16. Ambrose, "De Institutione Virginitate," *PL* 16:335.

17. Ambrose, "Exhortatio Virginitates," *PL* 16:359–60.

18. Ibid.

19. Joan Cadden, "Medieval Scientific and Medical Views of Sexuality: Questions of Propriety," *Medievalia et Humanistica*, n.s. 14 (1986), pp. 157–71.

20. Ambrose, Letter No. 32, in *Saint Ambrose: Letters*, pp. 154–60.

21. Ibid., p. 154.
22. Ambrose, "De Institutione Virginitate," *PL* 16:335.
23. Cyprian, "The Dress of Virgins," p. 33.
24. Ambrose, "De Institutione Virginitate," *PL* 16:345.
25. Ambrose, *On Virginity*, p. 13.
26. See Claude Chavasse, *The Bride of Christ: An Enquiry into the Nuptial Element in Early Christianity*, London 1940, p. 197, for the attribution of the Bride of Christ imagery to the Virgin Mary. See Bugge, p. 37, for the important association of virginity with an ontological wholeness that was seen as similar to the angelic life.
27. Ambrose, "De Lapsu Virginis Consecrate," *PL* 16:312.
28. Ambrose, "De Institutione Virginitate," *PL* 16:384.
29. Ambrose, *On Virginity*, p. 12.
30. Ambrose, "Exhortatio Virginitates," *PL* 16:353.
31. Jerome, "To Eustochium," p. 39.
32. "Concilium Eliberitanum, XII," *PL* 84:303. José M. Fernandez Caton, *Manifestaciones asceticas en la iglesia hispano-romano del siglo IV*, León 1962, p. 53, discusses this designation as a "public contract" which represented a significant change from early private commitments to chastity.
33. Jerome, "To Demetrias," p. 261.
34. Ambrose, *On Virginity*, p. 16.
35. Cyprian, "The Dress of Virgins," p. 47.
36. Jerome, "To Eustochium," pp. 27–8.
37. Ibid., p. 32.
38. Ibid., pp. 32–3.
39. Ambrose, Letter No. 32, *Letters*, p. 159.
40. Tertullian, "On the Apparel of Women," p. 130.
41. Ambrose, "Concerning Virgins," p. 375.
42. Jerome, "To Eustochium," p. 32.
43. Tertullian, "On the Veiling of Virgins," p. 35.
44. Ibid., p. 29.
45. Cyprian, "The Dress of Virgins," p. 35.
46. Jerome, "To Eustochium," p. 33.
47. Cyprian, "The Dress of Virgins," p. 35, says that no one, on seeing a virgin, should doubt that she is one.
48. Jerome, "To Demetrias," p. 271.
49. Jerome, "To Salvina," p. 167.
50. Jerome, "To Demetrias," p. 271.
51. For example, in Spain by the seventh century, when there were extremely well-established monastic communities for women, Jerome's letters were included in the *Codex Regularum*, a collection of readings that served as a rule for the monastery. Two such codices are the eleventh-century Escorial manuscript a II 9, and the tenth-century Escorial manuscript a I 13, copied by the nun Leodegúndia.
52. Jerome, "To Eustochium," pp. 32–3.
53. Jerome, "To Demetrias," p. 268.
54. Jerome, "To Eustochium," p. 28.
55. Jerome, "To Salvina," p. 166; "To Furia," p. 106.
56. Jerome, "To Eustochium," p. 25.
57. Jerome, "To Furia," p. 106.
58. Jerome, "To Eustochium," p. 28.
59. Jerome, "To Salvina," p. 166.
60. Jerome, "To Laeta," in *Nicene Fathers*, vol. VI, p. 194.
61. Jerome, "To Demetrias," p. 269.
62. Ibid., pp. 269–70. See also Cyprian, "The Dress of Virgins," p. 40.
63. Jerome, "To Rusticus," p. 249.
64. Jerome, "To Eustochium," p. 28.
65. Jerome, "To Laeta," p. 194.
66. Jerome, "To Eustochium," p. 35.

67. Jerome, "To Demetrias," p. 270.

68. Ambrose, "Concerning Virgins," p. 384; *On Virginity*, p. 23.

69. Jerome, "To Demetrias," p. 270; Tertullian, "On the Apparel of Women," p. 149.

70. Ambrose, "Concerning Virgins," p. 369.

71. Ambrose, "De Institutione Virginitate," *PL* 16:320, 327.

72. Ambrose, *On Virginity*, p. 27.

73. Ambrose, "Concerning Virgins," p. 382.

74. Ambrose, *On Virginity*, p. 5.

75. Jerome, "To Eustochium," p. 24.

76. Jerome, "Against Jovinian," p. 374.

77. Among the many references to bodies as "temples of God" are Ambrose, "De Lapsu Virginis Consecrate," *PL* 16:384, and Cyprian, "The Dress of Virgins," p. 32.

78. Ambrose, "Concerning Virgins," p. 376.

3 Augustine's Sexual Revolution

1. Current writers who have looked at Augustine's important contribution to the growth of sexual morality have acknowledged the Bishop's acceptance of sexuality. The best is Peter Brown, *The Body and Society*, New York 1988, pp. 387–428, but Brown's sensitive and learned analysis recoils from recognizing the degree to which Augustine defined lust and aberrant will with a particularly male expression of sexuality. Elizabeth Clark, "Vitiated Seeds and Holy Vessels: Augustine's Manichaean Past," in *Ascetic Piety and Women's Faith*, New York 1986, pp. 291–349, acknowledges the strong male identification with lust in Augustine by showing his location of original sin in the male seed.

2. Augustine, *The Retractions*, transl. Sister Mary Inez Bogan, Washington, 1968, p. 164.

3. Augustine, *The Catholic and Manichaean Ways of Life*, transl. D. A. Gallagher and I. J. Gallagher, Washington 1966, pp. 52–7.

4. Augustine, "Continence," in *Saint Augustine: Treatises on Various Subjects* (hereafter cited as *Treatises*), ed. R. J. Deferrari, New York 1952, p. 223.

5. Augustine, "Reply to Faustus the Manichaean," in *Nicene Fathers*, vol. IV, Buffalo 1887, pp. 326–7.

6. See Henry Chadwick, *Augustine*, New York 1986, p. 114.

7. Augustine, "The Good of Marriage," in *Saint Augustine: Treatises on Marriage and Other Subjects* (hereafter cited as *Treatises on Marriage*), transl. Charles T. Wilcox, New York 1955, p. 22.

8. Ibid., p. 209.

9. For a thorough discussion of the development of Augustine's thought on this matter, see Clark, "Vitiated Seeds," pp. 291–349.

10. Elaine Pagels, *Adam, Eve, and the Serpent*, New York 1988, pp. 105–26, discusses Augustine's dialogue with Julian, arguing that Augustine's views on sexuality led to limiting human freedom.

11. Augustine, "The Good of Marriage," pp. 38–9.

12. Ibid.

13. Jerome, "Against Jovinian," p. 368.

14. Augustine, *City of God*, XIV, 12, transl. H. Bettenson, Baltimore, MA 1972, p. 571.

15. Bugge, p. 115, noted that Augustine deemphasized the sexuality of original sin in favor of increasing the importance of pride. Bugge discusses the impact of this shift on the concept of virginity.

16. Augustine, *City of God*, XIV, 15, p. 575.

17. Ibid., p. 582.

18. Ibid., XIV, 26, p. 591.

19. Ibid., XIV, 16, p. 577.

20. Augustine, *Against Julian*, transl. M. A. Schumacher, New York 1957, p. 250.

21. Ibid., pp. 167–8.

22. Ibid., p. 144.

23. Ibid., p. 300.

24. Augustine, *City of God*, XIV, 19, p. 581.

25. Augustine, *Confessions*, p. 45. For an excellent description of Augustine's family life within the context of the late Empire, see B. D. Shaw, "The Family in Late Antiquity: The Experience of Augustine," *Past and Present*, 115, May 1987, pp. 3–51.

26. Augustine, "Continence," p. 197.

27. Ibid., p. 208.

28. Ibid., p. 213.

29. Ibid.

30. Augustine, in *The Retractions*, pp. 236, 259, describes his motivations for writing "On Marriage and Concupiscence" and *Against Julian*.

31. Clark, pp. 315–24.

32. Augustine, *Against Julian*, p. 119.

33. Ibid., p. 130.

34. Ibid., p. 148.

35. Ibid., p. 220.

36. Ibid., pp. 212–13.

37. Ibid., p. 219.

38. Ibid., p. 217.

39. Ibid., pp. 212–13.

40. Ibid., p. 127.

41. Augustine, *City of God*, XIV, 24, p. 587.

42. Augustine, *Against Julian*, p. 274.

43. Ibid., p. 274.

44. Augustine, *Against Julian*, p. 158.

45. Augustine, *City of God*, XIV, 24, p. 587.

46. Ibid., XIV, 16, p. 577.

47. Ibid., XIV, 26, p. 591.

48. Augustine, Sermon No. 214, in *Sermons on the Liturgical Seasons*, transl. Sister M. S. Muldowney, New York 1959, p. 136.

49. Augustine, "The Good of Marriage," p. 9.

50. Ibid., p. 12.

51. Ibid., pp. 47–8.

52. Ibid., p. 18.

53. Augustine, *Retractions*, p. 165.

54. Augustine, *Against Julian*, p. 202. See also "The Good of Marriage," p. 13.

55. Augustine, "Adulterous Marriage," in *Treatises on Marriage*, p. 117.

56. Augustine, "The Good of Marriage," p. 24.

57. Augustine, "De Moribus Mani," in *The Catholic and Manichaean Ways of Life*, pp. 109–10.

58. Brown, p. 390.

59. Bede, *Ecclesiastical History of the English People*, ed. B. Colgrave and R. A. B. Mynors, Oxford 1969, p. 97.

60. Augustine, "The Good of Marriage," p. 17.

61. Ibid., p. 63.

62. Ibid., p. 13.

63. Ibid., p. 25.

64. Augustine, *Against Julian*, p. 145.

65. Augustine, Sermon No. 205, p. 85.

66. Augustine, "Continence," p. 225.

67. Augustine, "The Good of Marriage," p. 13.

68. Ibid., p. 17.

69. Augustine, *Against Julian*, p. 228.

70. Augustine, *City of God*, XIV, 16, p. 577.

71. Augustine, "The Good of Marriage," p. 32.

72. Isidore of Seville, *Etymologias*, xvii, 7, 47, p. 351. For a general discussion of birth control during the late Empire, see Sarah B. Pomeroy, *Goddesses, Whores, Wives and Slaves*, New York 1975, p. 167.

73. Augustine, "The Good of Marriage," p. 25.

74. For summaries of later medieval attitudes toward sexual practices, see P. J. Payer, *Sex and the Penitentials*, Toronto 1984, and J. A. Brundage, "Let Me Count the Ways: Canonists and Theologians Contemplate Coital Positions," *Journal of Medieval History*, 10, 1984, pp. 81–92.

75. Augustine, "Adulterous Marriages," in *Treatises on Marriage*, p. 62.

76. Ibid., p. 130.

77. Ibid., p. 65.

78. Augustine, *City of God*, XIV, II, p. 570.

79. Augustine, "The Good of Marriage," p. 9.

80. Augustine, "The Good of Marriage," p. 34.

81. Augustine, "Continence," p. 216.

82. Augustine, *Against Julian*, p. 282.

83. Augustine, "The Good of Marriage," p. 28.

84. Augustine, *Confessions*, p. 169.

85. Ibid., pp. 177–8.

86. Augustine, *Against Julian*, p. 203.

87. Augustine, "Holy Virginity," in *Treatises on Marriage*, p. 166. See also "The Excellence of Widowhood," in *Treatises*, p. 284.

88. See Bugge, p. 134, where he describes Augustine's impact on the ideal of virginity: "The effect is a profound shift in emphasis from ontological ideal to ethical; what in Christian gnosis had referred more to a unique status of perfected being is transformed into merely visible evidence of a habitual state of the will."

89. Augustine, "Holy Virginity," pp. 174, 196; "Continence," p. 210.

90. "Holy Virginity," p. 184.

91. See Augustine, "The Excellence of Widowhood," pp. 304–5, for his use against the Pelagians of his position on the need for grace to achieve continence. For a clear and concise discussion of the dispute between Augustine and the Pelagians, see Henry Chadwick, *Augustine*, New York 1986, pp. 107–19.

92. Augustine, "Holy Virginity," p. 197.

93. Ibid., p. 184.

94. Augustine, "Reply to Faustus," p. 330.

95. Augustine, "Holy Virginity," p. 206. See also Augustine's summary of this treatise in *Retractions*, p. 167.

96. Augustine, "Holy Virginity," pp. 155, 167–8.

97. Augustine, "The Good of Marriage," p. 22. See Rosemary Radar, *Breaking Boundaries: Male/Female Friendship in Early Christian Communities*, New York 1983, for a discussion that demonstrates the accuracy of Augustine's observations.

98. Augustine, Letter No. 211, in *Letters: 204–270*, transl. Sister Wilfrid Parsons, New York 1956, pp. 41, 47.

99. Augustine, "The Excellence of Widowhood," p. 314.

100. Augustine, Letter No. 211, p. 44.

101. Augustine, "Holy Virginity," p. 184.

102. Augustine, Letter No. 211, p. 43.

103. Ibid.

104. Augustine, Letter No. 211, p. 50; "The Excellence of Widowhood," p. 313; *The Catholic and Manichaean Ways of Life*, p. 53.

105. Augustine, Letter No. 211, p. 50.

106. Ibid., p. 50.

107. Augustine, "The Good of Marriage," p. 45.

108. Augustine, Letter No. 266, in *Letters: 204–270*, p. 283.

PART II
The Virgins

4 Freedom from Social Expectations

1. Elaine Pagels, *Adam, Eve, and the Serpent*, p. 32.

2. Judith P. Hallett, *Fathers and Daughters in Roman Society*, Princeton, NJ 1984, pp. 109–10.

3. Ibid., pp. 136–43.

4. Esc. aII9 fol. 59. The whole narrative is between fol. 59 and 72. It is also in Paris MS. 2178, fols 207v to 219v.

5. Hallett, p. 102.

6. "Vita Ste Constantinae," Esc. aII9, fol. 60.

7. Ibid., fol. 60v.

8. Ibid., fol. 62.

9. Ibid., fol. 67.

10. Ibid., fol. 62.

11. See "De Sancto Gallicano," *Acta Sanctorum*, June, vol. 7, pp. 31-4; also Hroswitha of Gandersheim, "Gallicanus," in *The Plays of Roswitha*, transl. Christopher St John, London 1923, pp. 2–31.

12. "Vita Ste Constantinae," Esc. aII9, fol. 69v.

13. "De Sanctis Fratribus Martyribus Joanne et Paulo," *Acta Sanctorum*, June, vol. 7, pp. 138–42.

14. *Ammianus Marcellinus*, vol. I Book XIV, 1, 2, transl. John C. Rolfe, Cambridge 1963, p. 5.

15. See, for example, Sabine Baring-Gould, *Virgin Saints and Martyrs*, New York 1901, pp. 77–91. See also "De Sanctis Virginibus Romanis Constantia Augusta, Attica et Artemia," *Acta Sanctorum*, Feb. 18, vol. 3, p. 71.

16. There is even further confusion regarding this church. Christopher Hibbet, *Rome*, New York 1985, p. 78, argues that the Basilica of St Agnes was built by Constantine's granddaughter, Constantia Postuma. The dates make this impossible, but the conclusion derives from an inscription near the tomb of St Agnes that must refer to the granddaughter Constantia.

17. *Ammianus*, vol. II, XXI, 1, p. 93.

18. Baring-Gould, p. 83.

19. "De Sancto Gallicano," *Acta Sanctorum*, June, vol. 8, p. 32.

20. Aldhelm, *Aldhelm: The Poetic Works*, Exeter, Devon 1985, p. 99.

21. Ibid., pp. 148–50, for that section of the *Carmina* dealing with Constantina. The association of Constantina with Agnes appears on p. 146 of the *Carmina* within the narrative of Agnes.

22. Ibid., pp. 100–1.

23. Leah Lydia Otis, *Prostitution in Medieval Society*, Chicago 1985, p. 12.

24. Vern L. Bullough, *The History of Prostitution*, New York 1964, p. 48.

25. *The Theodosian Code*, 4, 6, 3, transl. Clyde Pharr, Princeton, NJ 1952, p. 86.

26. Romans 7:6.

27. For discussions of the various versions, see B. Bujila, *La Vie de Sainte Marie L'Egyptienne*, Ann Arbor, MI 1949; Peter F. Dembowski, *La Vie de Sainte Marie L'Egyptienne*, Geneva 1977; Michele Schiavone de Cruz-Saenz, *The Life of Saint Mary of Egypt*, Barcelona 1979.

28. See Dembowski, pp. 21–2, for a discussion of the expressions of these two elements in the various versions. J. R. Craddock, "Apuntos para el estudio de la legenda de santa Maria Egipciaca en España," *Homenaje a Rodriguez-Monino ... V. I*, Madrid 1966, p. 108, argues that there is a further dichotomy in the traditions: elite and popular. While this theory is very interesting, it needs further development.

29. "Vita Domne Marie Egiptie," Esc. aII9, fol. 126.

30. Bullough, p. 48.
31. G. L. Simons, *A Place for Pleasure: The History of the Brothel*, London 1975, p. 40.
32. "Vita Domne Marie Egiptie," fol. 126.
33. Ibid., fol. 127v.
34. M. K. Hopkins, "The Age of Roman Girls at Marriage," *Population Studies*, 18, 1965, p. 313.
35. "Vita Domne Marie Egiptie," fol. 127v. Chitty, p. 153, identifies this festival as the September feast of the Encaenia and the Exaltation of the Holy Cross. This was a major pilgrimage festival in the Eastern Empire.
36. "Vita Domne Marie Egiptie," fol. 127v.
37. Ibid., fol. 129.
38. Most of the versions put the length of her stay in the desert at forty-seven years. See, for example, Dembowski, p. 14, or Jacobus de Voragine, *Golden Legend*, transl. G. Ryan and H. Ripperger, New York 1969, pp. 228–30.
39. "Vita Domne Maria Egiptie," fol. 130.
40. Ibid., fol. 131v.
41. Ibid., fol. 132.

5 Freedom of Thought

1. G. Antolín, "Estudios de Codices Visigodos," *Boletín de la Real Academia de la Historia*, 86 (1925), p. 122.
2. Jerome, "To Theodora," in *Nicene Fathers*, vol. VI, p. 156.
3. These works, as well as other Jerome works circulated in Spain during the Visigothic era, are preserved in another tenth-century Visigothic manuscript, Escorial a I 13. The two writings praising virginity, "Against Jovinian" and "Against Helvidius," are also preserved in Esc. a II 9, just before the corpus of women's saints' Lives begins.
4. "Vita Sanctae Helia," Escorial MS. a II 9, fol. 73r.
5. Ibid., fol. 88v.
6. Ibid., fol. 92v.
7. Ibid., fol. 93r.
8. "Laus Ejusdem Virginem," Esc. a II 9, fol. 93r.
9. "Helia," fol. 90r.
10. Acts of Paul, in *The Apocryphal New Testament*, ed. M. Rhodes James, Oxford 1969, pp. 272–81.
11. Ibid., fol. 76r and 76v; Jerome, "Against Jovinian," pp. 361–3; "Against Helvidius," p. 344.
12. Jerome, "Against Jovinian," p. 364. See also "Helia," fol. 9lr. " ... from a virgin has grown virginity. ... "
13. Jerome, "Against Helividius," p. 344.
14. "Helia," fol. 83v.
15. Jerome, "Against Jovinian," p. 366.
16. "Helia," fol. 77v.
17. Ibid., fol. 83v.
18. Jerome, "To Eustochium," p. 23.
19. Jerome, "Against Jovinian," p. 374; see also Bugge, p. 20, for associations between sex and death, and thus conversely between virginity and life.
20. Jerome, "Against Jovinian," p. 360; "Helia," fol. 89v.
21. Jerome, "To Pammachius," in *Nicene Fathers*, vol. VI, p. 71.
22. "Helia," fol. 75r.
23. Ibid., fol. 89r.
24. Ibid.
25. The biblical examples used by Helia's mother in support of a married life were taken from Jerome, "Against Jovinian," pp. 348–9 and "Against Helvidius," p. 344. They may be found in the *Vita* on fol. 74r.

26. "Helia," fols 74v, 75r; Jerome, "To Pammachius," p. 71.
27. Jerome, "To Eustochium," p. 29.
28. "Helia," fol. 9lr.
29. Ibid., fol. 90r.
30. Ibid., fol. 91v.
31. Ibid., fol. 9lr.
32. Jerome, "Against Helvidius," p. 344.
33. I John 5: 7–8.
34. "Helia," fol. 75r.
35. "Helia," fol. 79r.
36. Jerome, "To Eustochium," p. 29.
37. "Helia," fol. 89r.
38. Jerome, "Against Jovinian," p. 367.
39. "Helia," fol. 80r.
40. "Helia," fol. 85r; Jerome, "Against Jovinian," p. 355; "To Eustochium," p. 30.
41. Jerome, "To Eustochium," p. 31.
42. Ibid., p. 39.
43. "Helia," fol. 84r.
44. Jerome, "To Eustochium," p. 35.
45. "Helia," fol. 74r.
46. Jerome, "To Eustochium," p. 33.

6 Freedom of Movement

1. Jerome, "To Eustochium," p. 32.
2. See E. D. Hunt, *Holy Land Pilgrimage in the Later Roman Empire AD 312–46*, Oxford 1982, for a good description of this sort of pilgrimage.
3. We should remember also that at least by the sixth century the Western Church was not comfortable with holy men traveling around either. See, for example, *The Rule of Saint Benedict*, transl. Cardinal Gasquet, New York 1966, p. 8; and for Spain, see the Fourth Council of Toledo, canon 52 in "Concilia Hispaniae," *PL* 84:378.
4. Elizabeth A. Clark, transl., *The Life of Melania the Younger*, New York 1984; John Wilkinson, *Egeria's Travels*, London 1971; George E. Gingras, transl., *Egeria: Diary of a Pilgrimage*, New York 1970.
5. There has been much controversy over the probable dates of Egeria's pilgrimage. The most convincing argument for these dates may be found in P. Devos, "La Date du Voyage D'Egerie," *Analecta Bollandiana*, 85, 1967, pp. 163–94. For a summary of the arguments on the dating, see Wilkinson, pp. 237–39.
6. Wilkinson, pp. 95, 98, 121, 122.
7. Ibid., p. 94.
8. Ibid., p. 97.
9. Ibid., p. 120.
10. Ibid., p. 113.
11. Ibid., pp. 94, 111 for two examples. See Hunt, pp. 130–31, for a discussion of these holy souvenirs.
12. Wilkinson, p. 113.
13. Ibid., pp. 94, 118.
14. Ibid., pp. 93, 106.
15. Hunt, p. 164, suggests that since the Emperor Theodosius was from Spain, Egeria may have been related to him or at least have known some of the many Spaniards in his court.
16. Wilkinson, pp. 115, 118.
17. Ibid., pp. 101, 103.
18. Ibid., pp. 98, 101, 105, 121.
19. Ibid., p. 120.

20. Jerome, "To Furia," p. 106.

21. Morin, D. B. "Un passage énigmatique de S. Jérome contre la pèlerine espagnole Eucheria?," *Revue Bénédictine* 30 (1913), pp. 181–4.

22. J. N. D. Kelly, *Jerome: His Life, Writings and Controversies*, London 1975, p. 191.

23. "Epistola de B. Echeria," Escorial MS. a II 9, fol. 118v. For a published edition of this text see "Sancti Valerii Abbatis, opuscula," *PL* 87:421–5. Wilkinson has provided an English translation in *Egeria's Travels*, pp. 174–8.

24. For a fascinating account of Valerius's life as a holy man on the edges of society, see Sister Consuelo Maria Aherne, transl., *Valerio of Bierzo: An Ascetic of the Late Visigothic Period*, Washington 1949.

25. See Clark, *Melania*, pp. 83–92, for a full discussion of Melania's family.

26. "Vita Sanctae Melaniae," Escorial MS. a II 9, fol. 94v.

27. Ibid., fol. 97v.

28. Ibid. See Clark, *Melania*, pp. 95–104, for a discussion of Melania's and Pinian's wealth.

29. "Vita Sanctae Melaniae," fol. 96v.

30. Ibid., fol. 97v.

31. Ibid., fol. 99.

32. Ibid.

33. Ibid.

34. Ibid., fol. 100v.

35. Ibid.

36. Ibid., fol. 101.

37. Ibid., fol. 103.

38. Ibid.

39. Ibid., fol. 106.

40. Ibid., fol. 106v. The Latin manuscript has Melania preaching only to women, while the Greek draws no such distinction. I believe this is an example of the Latin editor's attempt to bring the *Vita* into line with patristic recommendations.

41. Ibid., fol. 108v.

42. Ibid., fol. 111.

43. Clark, *Melania*, p. 23, suggests that the story was added to discredit the Empress, who was a Monophysite supporter. This seems unlikely owing to the unrelatedness of the incident with Monophysite thought. In fact, the incident is about enclosure, so it seems simplest and most obvious to assume that it is commenting on this.

44. "Sanctae Melaniae," fol. 111v. This, too, was added in the Latin version, probably to conform to Latin custom. See Clark, *Melania*, p. 194.

45. "Sanctae Melaniae," fol. 112.

46. Ibid.

7 Freedom from Gender Identification

1. Jerome, "To Eustochium," p. 34.

2. Acts of Paul and Thecla, in James, *The Apocryphal New Testament*, pp. 272–96.

3. Ambrose, "Concerning Virgins," p. 378.

4. Ambrose, Letter No. 78, in Beyenke, p. 435. For the biblical prohibition, see Deuteronomy 22.5.

5. Brundage, *Law, Sex, and Christian Society*, p. 108.

6. This Life may be found in Esc. a II 9, fols. 120 to 124v.

7. The Church of St Julian was on the outskirts of Antioch. It was certainly built sometime before the year 444 (Julian had died about 380). The church was destroyed by the Persians in 573. See Glanville Downey, *Ancient Antioch*, Princeton, NJ 1963, p. 259; and G. Downey, *A History of Antioch in Syria*, Princeton, NJ 1961, p.545, for a discussion of the history of this church. The mention of a destroyed church in the Life strongly

suggests that the Life was written while the church still stood, thus arguing for a fairly contemporary narrative.

8. "Vitae Sanctae Pelagiae" Esc. a II 9, fol. 120v.

9. Ibid., fol. 121.

10. Ibid., fol. 121v.

11. Ibid., fol. 122.

12. Ibid., fol. 122v.

13. See C.A. Luttrell, "The Medieval Tradition of the Pearl Virginity," *Medium Aevum*, 31, pp. 194–200, for the extensive association between pearls and virginity.

14. Jerome, "To Eustochium," p. 24.

15. "Vitae Sanctae Pelagiae," fol. 123.

16. Ibid., fol. 123v.

17. Ibid.

18. See Clark, *Melania the Younger*, p. 116.

19. "Vita Sanctae Pelagiae," fol. 124.

20. Ibid., fol. 124.

21. See Agnes Smith Lewis, *Select Narratives of Holy Women: Syriac Text. Studia Sinaitica X*, London 1900. The Life is more easily accessible in Agnes Smith Lewis, "The Life of Euphrosyne of Alexandria," *Vox Benedictina*, July 1984, pp. 140–56.

22. "Vita Sanctae Castissimae," Esc. MS. a II 9, fol. 113.

23. Ibid., fol. 113v.

24. P. R. Coleman-Norton, ed., *Roman State and Christian Church: A Collection of Legal Documents to AD 535*, London 1966, pp. 430–31.

25. "Vita Sanctae Castissimae," Esc. a II 9, fol. 114.

26. Ibid., fol. 114.

27. Gertrude Jobes, *Dictionary of Mythology, Folklore and Symbols*, New York 1962, p. 508; Maria Leach, ed., *Standard Dictionary of Folklore, Mythology and Legend*, San Francisco 1972, p. 344.

28. "Vita Sanctae Castissimae," fol. 114.

29. Ibid., fol. 114v.

30. Ibid., fol. 115.

31. Ibid., fol. 115.

32. Ibid., fol. 115v.

33. Ibid., fol. 116.

34. Jobes, p. 508.

35. Hermann Usener, *Legenden der Heiligen Pelagia*, Bonn 1879.

36. Marie Delcourt, *Hermaphrodite: Myths and Rites of the Bisexual Figure in Classical Antiquity*, transl. Jennifer Nicholson, London 1961, pp. 96, 99.

37. John Anson, "The Female Transvestite in Early Monasticism: The Origin and Development of a Motif," *Viator*, 5, 1974, p. 18.

38. Ibid., p. 30.

39. Ibid., p. 17.

40. Wayne Meeks, "Image of the Androgyne: Some Uses of a Symbol in Earliest Christianity," *History of Religions*, 3, February 1974, p. 197. For further associations of Gnosticism with androgyny, see Radar, p. 41, and Elaine Pagels, *Gnostic Gospels*, New York 1981, pp. 57–83.

41. See Vern Bullough, "Transvestites in the Middle Ages," *American Journal of Sociology*, 79, 1974, pp. 1381–94, where he argues that this issue of cross-dressing was primarily one of status. Women gained status when they dressed as men, so they did it; men lost status if they dressed as women, so they did not do it.

8 The Virgins on Sexuality and Virginity

1. Palladius, *The Lausiac History*, transl. Robert T. Meyer, London 1965, pp. 36–7.

2. "Vita Sanctae Heliae," Esc. a II 9, fol. 91.

3. "Vita Sanctae Melaniae," Esc. a II 9, fol. 109.

4. "Vitae Sanctae Constantinae," fol. 64v.

5. "Vita Sanctae Constantinae," Esc. a II 9, fol. 60v.

6. Ibid.

7. "Vita Domne Marie Egiptie," Esc. a II 9. fol. 125.

8. "Vita Sanctae Melaniae," Esc. a II 9, fol. 109.

9. "Vita Sanctae Constantina," Esc. a II 9. fol. 60v.

10. Rosemary Radar, *Breaking Boundaries: Male/Female Friendship in Early Christian Communities*, New York 1983, p. 61.

11. Ibid., p. 109.

12. This same argument is sometimes made today. See, for example, V. S. Finn, "Two Ways of Loving," in *Celibate Loving*, ed. Mary Anne Huddleston, New York 1984, pp. 29–45, where she argues that a friendship without sex provides intimacy with freedom. On the other hand, a friendship with sex provides intimacy without freedom.

13. Jerome, "To Eustochium," p. 25; "Vita Domne Marie Egiptie," Esc. a II 9, fol. 129v.

14. "Vita Sanctae Melaniae," Esc. a II 9, fol 99.

15. Ibid., fol. 104.

16. "Vita Sanctae Castissimae," Esc. a II 9, fol. 113.

17. "Vita Sanctae Pelagiae," Esc. a II 9, fol. 123.

18. "Vita Sanctae Melaniae," Esc. a II 9, fol. 97v.

19. Simone de Beauvoir, *The Second Sex*, transl. H. M. Parshley, New York 1968, p. 96.

20. Livy, *From the Founding of the City*, Book xxxiv, transl. Evan T. Sage, Cambridge, MA 1961, pp. 413–39.

21. Ibid., p. 437.

22. Bullough, *The History of Prostitution*, New York 1964, p. 48.

23. "Vita Sanctae Melaniae," Esc. a II 9, fol. 96v.

24. Ibid., fol. 100v.

25. There is abundant literature on the purposes and meaning of clothing, but a good, readable survey on the subject may be found in Alison Lurie, *The Language of Clothes*, New York 1981.

26. "Vita Sanctae Melaniae," Esc. a II 9, fol. 112.

27. "Vita Domne Marie Egiptie," Esc. a II 9, fol. 130.

28. "Vita Sanctae Constantinae", Esc. a II 9, fol. 60v.

29. "Vita Sanctae Castissimae," Esc. a II 9, fol. 113v.

30. "Vita Sanctae Constantinae," Esc. a II 9, fol. 62.

31. "Vita Sanctae Constantinae," Esc. a II 9, fol. 61v.

32. "Vita Sanctae Melaniae," Esc. a II 9, fol.108v.

33. "Vitae Sanctae Constantinae," Esc. a II 9, fol. 63.

34. "Vita Sanctae Melaniae," Esc. a II 9, fol. 103.

35. Ibid., fol. 103v.

36. Ibid., fol. 104. The Latin version of the Life of Melania adds another discussion of obedience that is not in the Greek Life. In this version, obedience is seen in the hierarchy of bishops under the "prince of bishops," who in turn owes obedience to the synod. Since this view of obedience is inconsistent with all of Melania's other speeches and actions, I believe it was added by the Latin editor of the Greek Life to try to bring the Life into more conformity with patristic, hierarchic thought rather than the ascetic tradition. See Clark, *Melania the Younger*, p. 191.

37. "Vitae Sanctae Constantinae," Esc. a II 9, fol. 70.

38. "Vitae Sanctae Castissimae," Esc. a II 9, fol. 112v.

39. Wilkinson, p. 120.

40. "Vita Sanctae Melaniae," Esc. a II 9, fol. 99.

41. "Vita Domne Marie Egiptie," Esc. a II 9, fol. 128.

42. "Vitae Sanctae Constantinae," Esc. a II 9, fol. 66-66v.

43. "Vita Sanctae Melaniae," Esc. a II 9, fols 110v, 106v.

44. Palladius, p. 17.

45. Ambrose, "Concerning Virgins," *Nicene Fathers*, vol. X, p. 380.
46. McNamara, *A New Song*, pp. 2–3.
47. Tertullian, "On the Veiling of Virgins," p. 33.
48. Ibid., p. 28.

Appendix

The Manuscript Tradition

1. Ildephonse of Toledo, "De Viris Illustribus" IV, in *PL* 96:200.

2. Guillermo Antolín, "Vida de Santa Helia," Boletín de la Academía de la Historia 55, 1909, p. 122. See also Joyce E. Salisbury, *Iberian Popular Religion, 600 BC to 700 AD*, New York 1985, pp. 202–3.

3. See J. R. Craddock, "Apuntos para el estudio de la leyenda de santa Maria Egipciaca en España," *Homenaje a Rodriguez-Monino* ... v. 1, 1966, p. 99–110, for a discussion of the manuscript tradition and early redactions of the Life.

4. Craddock, p. 102.

5. Cardonal Rampolla del Tindaro, *Santa Melania Guiniore Senatrice Romana*, Rome 1908, p. xlvi.

6. P. Guillermo Antolín, *Un Codex Regularum del Siglo ix*, Madrid 1908, p. 5.

7. Cardinal Rampolla studied the important Iberian tradition of the Life of Melania but did not know of this manuscript, so his stemma needs to be revised to incorporate it.

8. **a** fol. 186v.

9. Antolín, *Un Codex Regularum*, p. 16, advocates this date.

10. M. C. Díaz y Díaz, "El Códice Monastico de Leodegúndia (a I 13)", *Cuidad de Dios*, 181, 1968, p. 571, advocates this date.

11. **a** fol. 126v; **b** fol. 95; **c** fol. 241v.

12. **a** fol. 133; **b** fol. 100v; **c** fol. 248.

13. **a** fol. 128; **b** fol. 96; **c** fol. 243. I want to acknowledge the help of Robert Wojtowicz, who worked as my research assistant and helped to collate the Melania texts.

14. **b** fol. 132v reveals the name of the scribe and the date of the copy.

15. **a** fol. 126; **b** fol. 94; **c** fol. 241.

16. **a** fol. 138v; **b** fol. 106; **c** fol. 253.

17. See **a** fol. 139v; **b** fol. 106v; **c** fol. 253v.

18. See Craddock for a discussion of this vernacular tradition.

Bibliography

Aherne, Sister Consuelo Maria, *Valerio of Bierzo: An Ascetic of the Late Visigothic Period. Series in Medieval History, New Series, vol. xi.* Washington: The Catholic University Press, 1949.

Aldhelm, *Aldhelm: The Poetic Works,* transl. M. Lapidge and J. L. Rosier. Exeter, Devon: Short Run Press Ltd, 1985.

Ambrogio, Sant, *Scritti Sulla Verginita,* transl. M. Salvati. Turin: Societa Editrice Internazionale, 1955.

Ambrose, *On Virginity,* transl. Daniel Callam. Saskatoon, SK: Peregrina Publishing, 1980.

Ambrose, "De Lapsu Virginis Consecrate," *PL* 16: 383–400.

Ambrose, *Saint Ambrose: Letters,* transl. Sister Mary Melchior Beyenke. New York: Fathers of the Church, 1954.

Ambrose, "De Virginitate," *PL* 16: 279–318.

Ambrose, *A Select Library of Nicene and Post-Nicene Fathers,* vol. X, ed. P. Schaff and H. Wace. New York: Christian Literature Co., 1895.

Ambrose, "Exhortatio Virginitatis," *PL* 16: 351–80.

Ambrose, "Expositio Evangeliis Secundum Lucam," *PL* 15: 1527–1850.

Ambrose, "De Institutione Virginitate," *PL* 16: 319–48.

Ammianus Marcellinus, *Ammianus Marcellinus.* transl. John C. Rolfe. Cambridge, MA: Harvard University Press, 1963.

Anson, John, "The Female Transvestite in Early Monasticism: The Origin and Development of a Motif," *Viator* 5 (1974), pp. 1–32.

Antolín, P. Guillermo, "Historia Y Descripcion de un 'Codex Regularum' del siglo IX," *Ciudad de Dios,* LXXV (1908).

Antolín P. Guillermo, *Un Codex Regularum del Siglo ix.* Madrid: Imp. Helenica Real Biblioteca del Escorial, 1908.

Antolín, P. Guillermo, *Catalogo de los Codices Latinos de la Real Biblioteca del Escorial vol. I.* Madrid, 1910.

Antolín, P. Guillermo. "Estudios de Codices Visigodos," *Boletin de la Real Academia de la Historia,* 86 (1925), pp. 54–315, 605–38.

Ariès, Philippe and Béjin, André, eds, *Western Sexuality: Practice & Precept in Past and Present Times.* Oxford: Basil Blackwell, 1985.

Augustine, *The Retractions*, transl. Sister Mary Inez Bogan. Washington: Catholic University of America Press, 1968.

Augustine, *The Confessions*, transl. R. S. Pine-Coffin. New York: Penguin, 1980.

Augustine, *Against Julian*, transl. Matthew A. Schumacher. New York: Fathers of the Church, Inc., 1957.

Augustine, *Saint Augustine: Treatises on Marriage and Other Subjects*, transl. Charles T. Wilcox *et al.* New York: Fathers of the Church, Inc., 1955.

Augustine, *Saint Augustine: Treatises on Various Subjects*, ed. R. J. Deferrari. New York: Fathers of the Church, Inc., 1952.

Augustine, *Saint Augustine: Letters, vol. V*, transl. Sister Wilfrid Parsons. New York: Fathers of the Church, Inc., 1956.

Augustine, "Reply to Faustus the Manichaean," in *The Nicene and Post-Nicene Fathers, First Series*, vol. IV. Buffalo: Christian Literature Co., 1887.

Augustine, *The Catholic and Manichaean Ways of Life*, transl. D. A. Gallagher and I.J. Gallagher. Washington: Catholic University of America Press, 1966.

Augustine, *Sermons on the Liturgical Season*, transl. Sister Mary Sarah Muldowney. New York: Fathers of the Church, Inc., 1959.

Augustine, *Concerning the City of God Against the Pagans*, transl. H. Bettenson. Baltimore, MD: Penguin, 1972.

Bailey, Derrick Sherwin, *Sexual Relations in Christian Thought*. New York: Harper & Brothers, 1959.

Balsdon, J.P.V.D., *Roman Women*. London: The Bodley Head, 1962.

Baring-Gould, Sabine, *The Lives of the Saints*. London: John C. Nimmo, 1897.

Baring-Gould, Sabine, *Virgin Saints and Martyrs*. New York: Thomas Y. Crowell & Co., 1901.

Barnes, Timothy David, *Tertullian: A Historical and Literary Study*. Oxford: Clarendon Press, 1971.

Basil the Great, *The Treatise de Spiritu Sancto; The Nine Homilies of the Hexaemeron and the Letters*, transl. Rev. Blomfield Jackson. New York: Christian Literature Co., 1895.

Beauvoir, Simone de, *The Second Sex*, transl. H. M. Parshley. New York: The Modern Library, 1968.

Bede, *Bede's Ecclesiastical History of the English People*, ed. B. Colgrave and R.A.B. Mynors. Oxford: Clarendon Press, 1969.

Benedict, *The Rule of Saint Benedict*, transl. Cardinal Gasquet. New York: Cooper Square Publishers, Inc., 1966.

Bibliotheca Hagiographica Orientalis, ed. Socii Bollandiani. Brussels, 1910.

Borreson, Kari, *Subordination and Equivalence: The Nature and Role of Women in Augustine and Thomas Aquinas*. Washington: Catholic University of America Press, 1981.

Brown, Peter R. L., *Augustine of Hippo: A Biography*. Berkeley, CA: University of California Press, 1967.

Brown, Peter R. L., "The Rise and Function of the Holy Man in Late Antiquity," *Journal of Roman Studies* 61 (1971), pp. 80–101.

Brown, Peter R. L., *Religion and Society in the Age of Saint Augustine*. New York: Harper & Row, 1972.

Brown, Peter R. L., *The Cult of the Saints.* Chicago: University of Chicago Press, 1981.

Brown, Peter R. L., "Augustine and Sexuality," *Protocol of the Colloquy of the Center for Hermeneutical Studies* ... Berkeley, CA: Center for Hermeneutical Studies, 1983.

Brown, Peter R. L., *The Body and Society: Men, Women, and Sexual Renunciation in Early Christianity.* New York: Columbia University Press, 1988.

Brundage, James A., "Let Me Count the Ways: Canonists and Theologians Contemplate Coital Positions," *Journal of Medieval History* 10 (1984), pp. 81–93.

Brundage, James A., *Law, Sex, and Christian Society in Medieval Europe.* Chicago: University of Chicago Press, 1987.

Bugge, J., *Virginitas: An Essay in the History of a Medieval Ideal.* The Hague: Martinus Nijhoff, 1975.

Bujila, Bernadine, *La Vie de Sainte Marie L'Egyptienne.* Ann Arbor, MI: Michigan University Press, 1949.

Bullough, Vern L., *The History of Prostitution.* New York: University Books, 1964.

Bullough, Vern L., *The Subordinate Sex: A History of Attitudes Toward Women.* Urbana, IL, 1973.

Bullough, Vern L., "Medieval Medical and Scientific Views of Women," *Viator* 4 (1973), pp. 485–501.

Bullough, Vern L., "Transvestites in the Middle Ages," *American Journal of Sociology* 79 (1974), pp. 1381–94.

Bullough, Vern L., "Sex Education in Medieval Christianity," *Journal of Sex Research* XIII (1977), pp. 185–96.

Bullough, Vern L. and Brundage, James, *Sexual Practices and the Medieval Church.* New York: Prometheus Books, 1982.

Burrus, Virginia, *Chastity as Autonomy: Women in the Stories of Apocryphal Acts.* New York: Edwin Mellen Press, 1987.

Butler, Alban, *Lives of the Saints,* ed. H. Thurston and D. Attwater. New York: Kenedy, 1963.

Cadden, Joan, "Medieval Scientific and Medical Views of Sexuality: Questions of Propriety," *Medievalia et Humanistica,* n.s. 14 (1986), pp. 157–71.

Castelli, Elizabeth, "Virginity and its Meaning for Women's Sexuality in Early Christianity," *Journal of Feminist Studies in Religion* 2: 1 (Spring 1986), pp. 61–88.

Catalogus Codicum Hagiographicorum Latinorum Antiquiorum Saeculo XVI qui Asservantur in Bibliotheca Nationali Parisiense, ed. Hagiographi Bollandiani. Brussels, 1893.

Catholic Encyclopedia. New York: McGraw-Hill, 1967–79.

Chadwick, Henry, *Augustine.* New York: Oxford University Press, 1986.

Chavasse, Claude, *The Bride of Christ: An Enquiry into the Nuptial Element in Early Christianity.* London: Faber & Faber, 1940.

Chitty, Dervas J., *The Desert a City: An Introduction to the Study of Egyptian and Palestinian Monasticism under the Christian Empire.* Oxford: Basil Blackwell, 1966.

Chrysostom, John, *On Virginity: Against Remarriage*, transl. S. R. Shore. New York: Edwin Mellen Press, 1983.

Church, F. Forrester, "Sex and Salvation in Tertullian," *Harvard Theological Review* 68 (April 1975), pp. 83–101.

Clark, Elizabeth, *Jerome, Chrysostem & Friends*. New York: Edwin Mellen Press, 1979.

Clark, Elizabeth, *Women in the Early Church*. Wilmington, DE: Glazier, 1983.

Clark, Elizabeth, transl., *The Life of Melania the Younger*. New York: Edwin Mellen Press, 1984.

Clark, Elizabeth, *Ascetic Piety and Women's Faith*. New York: Edwin Mellen Press, 1986.

Coleman-Norton, P. R., ed., *Roman State and Christian Church: A Collection of Legal Documents to AD 535*. London: SPCK, 1966.

Concilia Hispaniae, *PL* 84, 301 ff.

Craddock, J. R., "Apuntos para el estudio de la leyenda de santa Maria Egipciaca en España," *Homenaje a Rodriguez-Monino* ... V. 1. (1966), pp. 99–110.

Cyprian, *Saint Cyprian: Treatises*. transl. Roy J. Deferrari. New York: Fathers of the Church, Inc., 1958.

Davies, Stevan L., *The Revolt of the Widows: The Social World of the Apocryphal Acts*. Carbondale, IL: Southern Illinois University Press, 1980.

De S. Pelagia, *Acta Sanctorum* October, vol. 4, pp. 248–68.

De Sanctis Virginibus Romanis Constantia Augusta, Attica et Artemia, *Acta Sanctorum*, February, vol. 3, pp. 67–72.

De Sancto Gallicano, *Acta Sanctorum*, June, vol. 7, pp. 31–4.

De Sanctis Fratribus Martyribus Joanne et Paulo, *Acta Sanctorum*, June, vol. 7, pp. 138–42.

Delehaye, Hippolyte, "Les Femmes Stylites," *Analecta Bollandiana* 27 (1908), pp. 391–2.

Delcourt, Marie, *Hermaphrodite: Myths and Rites of the Bisexual Figure in Classical Antiquity*, transl. Jennifer Nicholson. London: Studio, 1961.

Delmas, F., "Remarques sur la vie de sainte Marie l'Egyptienne," *Echos d'Orient* IV (1900), pp. 35–42.

Delmas, F. "Encore Sainte Marie L'Egyptienne," *Echos d'Orient* V (1901), pp. 15–17.

Dembowski, Peter F., *La Vie de Sainte Marie L'Egyptienne*. Geneva: Librairie Droz, 1977.

Devos, P., "La Date du Voyage D'Egerie," *Analecta Bollandiana* 85 (1967), pp. 165–94; 86 (1968), pp. 87–108.

Díaz y Díaz, Dr M. C., "El Códice Monastico de Leodegúndia (a I 13)," *Ciudad de Dios* 181 (1968), p. 567.

Dillard, Heath, *Daughters of the Reconquest: Women in Castilian Town Society, 1100–1300*. Cambridge: University Press, 1985.

Dooley, William Joseph, *Marriage According to St Ambrose*. Washington: Catholic University of America Press, 1948.

Downey, Glanville, *A History of Antioch in Syria*. Princeton, NJ: University Press, 1961.

Downey, Glanville, *Ancient Antioch.* Princeton, NJ: University Press, 1963.

Dumm, Demetrius, *The Theological Basis of Virginity According to St Jerome.* Latrobe, PA: St Vincent Archabbey, 1961.

Etheria, *The Pilgrimage of Etheria,* transl. M. L. McClure & C. L. Feltoe. New York: Macmillan, 1919.

Eusebius Pamphilus, *The Life of Constantine.* London: Samuel Bagster & Sons, 1845.

Evdokin, Paul, *The Sacrament of Love: The Nuptial Mystery in the Light of Orthodox Tradition,* transl. A. Gythiel and V. Steadman. Crestwood, NY: St Vladimir's Seminary Press, 1985.

Fernandez Caton, José M., *Manifestaciones asceticas en la iglesia hispano-romano del siglo IV.* León: Archivo Historico Diocesano, 1962.

Ferotin, M., "Le véritable auteur de la 'Peregrinatio Silviae,' la vierge espagnole Etheria," *Revue des questions historiques* 74 (1903), pp. 367–97.

Flugel, J. C., *The Psychology of Clothes.* London: The Hogarth Press, 1950.

Frend, W. H. C., *The Rise of Christianity.* Philadelphia: Fortress Press, 1984.

Gasquet, Cardinal, transl., *The Rule of St Benedict.* New York: Cooper Square Publishers, Inc., 1966.

Gingras, George E., transl. *Egeria: Diary of a Pilgrimage.* New York: Newman Press, 1970.

Giordani, I., *The Social Message of the Early Church Fathers,* transl. Alba I. Zizzania. Paterson, NJ: St Anthony Guild Press, 1944.

Gorce, D., ed., *Vie de Sainte Melania, Sources Chrétiens, 90.* Paris: Les Editions du Cerf, 1962.

Hallett, Judith P., *Fathers and Daughters in Roman Society.* Princeton, NJ: University Press, 1984.

Harkx, Peter, *The Fathers on Celibacy.* De Pere, WI: St Norbert Abbey Press, 1968.

Hibbet, Christopher, *Rome.* New York: Norton, 1985.

Hopkins, M. K., "The Age of Roman Girls at Marriage," *Population Studies* 18 (1965), pp. 309–27.

Hroswitha of Gandersheim, *The Plays of Roswitha,* transl. Christopher St John. London: Chatto & Windus, 1923.

Huddleston, Mary Anne, *Celibate Loving.* New York: Paulist Press, 1984.

Hunt, E. D., *Holy Land Pilgrimage in the later Roman Empire AD 312–46.* Oxford: University Press, 1982.

Ildephonse of Toledo, "De Viris Illustribus," *PL* 96: 202.

Isidore of Seville, "De Viduis," "De Conjugatis," "De Ecclesiasticus Officiis, Lib. II," *PL* 83: pp. 807–12.

Isidore of Seville, *Etimologias, vols I & II,* ed. J. Oroz Reta and Manuel Marcos Casquero. Madrid: Biblioteca de Autores Cristianos, 1982.

Isidore of Seville, *Etymologiarum sive originum libri xx,* ed. W. M. Lindsay. Oxford: Clarendon Press, 1911.

Jacobus de Voragine, *The Golden Legend,* transl. G. Ryan and H. Ripperger. New York: Arno Press, 1969.

James, M. R., transl. *The Apocryphal New Testament.* Oxford: Clarendon Press, 1969.

Jerome, *A Select Library of Nicene and Post-Nicene Fathers, V. VI*, ed. P. Schaff and H. Wace. New York: Christian Literature Co., 1893.

Jerome, "Commentariorum in Epistolam ad Ephesios libri III," *PL* 26: 459–554.

Jobes, Gertrude, *Dictionary of Mythology, Folklore and Symbols.* New York: The Scarecrow Press, Inc., 1962.

Kelly, J.N.D., *Jerome: His Life, Writings and Controversies.* London: Duckworth, 1975.

King, Margot H., *The Desert Mothers: A Survey of the Feminine Anchoretical Tradition.* Saskatoon, SK: Peregrina Publishing Co., 1984.

Kraemer, Ross, "The Conversion of Women to Ascetic Forms of Christianity," *Signs* VI (1980/81), pp. 298–307.

Laeuchli, Samuel, *Power and Sexuality. The Emergence of Canon Law at the Synod of Elvira.* Philadelphia: Temple University Press, 1972.

LaPorte, Jean, *The Role of Women in Early Christianity.* New York: Edwin Mellen Press, 1982.

Le Noin de Tillemont, Louis S., *Memoires, pour servir à l'Histoire ecclésiastique des six premiers siècles* ... Paris: Robustel, 1701–6.

Leach, Maria, ed., *Standard Dictionary of Folklore, Mythology and Legend.* San Francisco: Harper & Row, 1972.

Leage, R. W., *Roman Private Law.* London, 1930.

Leclercq, H. "Marie L'Egyptienne," in *Dictionnaire d'archéologie chrétienne et de liturgie x, 2 partie.* Paris: Libraire Letouzey et Ane, 1932, col. 2128–36.

Livy, *From the Founding of the City*, transl. Evan T. Sage. Cambridge, MA: Harvard University Press, 1961.

Loomis, C. Grant, *White Magic: An Introduction to the Folklore of Christian Legend.* Cambridge, MA: Medieval Academy of America, 1948.

Lucas, Angela M., *Women in the Middle Ages: Religion, Marriage and Letters.* New York: St Martin's Press, 1983.

Lurie, Alison, *The Language of Clothes.* New York: Random House, 1981.

Luttrell, C. A., "The Medieval Tradition of the Pearl Virginity," *Medium Aevum* (31), pp. 194–200.

McNamara, Jo Ann, "Sexual Equality and the Cult of Virginity in Early Christian Thought," *Feminist Studies* 3 (1976), pp. 145–58.

McNamara, Jo Ann, *A New Song: Celibate Women in the First Three Christian Centuries.* New York: Haworth, 1983.

McNamara, Jo Ann, "Muffled Voices: The Lives of Consecrated Women in the Fourth Century," in *Distant Echoes*, ed. John A. Nichols and L. T. Shank. Kalamazoo, MI: Cistercian Publications, Inc., 1984.

Markele, Jean, *Women of the Celts.* London: Gordon Cremonesi, 1975.

Meeks, Wayne, "Image of the Androgyne: Some Uses of a Symbol in Earliest Christianity," *History of Religions* 3 (1974), pp. 165–208.

Miles, Margaret R., *Augustine on the Body.* Missoula, MT: Scholars Press, 1979.

Morgan, James, *The Importance of Tertullian in the Development of Christian Dogma.* London: Kegan Paul, Trench, Trubner & Co., 1928.

Morin, D. B., "Un passage énigmatique de S. Jérome contre La pèlerine Éspagnole Eucheria?", *Revue Bénédictine* 30 (1913), pp. 174–86.

Morin, G., "Deux lettres mystiques d'une ascète espagnole," *Revue Benedictine*

40 (1928), pp. 293–303.

Mullins, Sister Patrick Jerome, *The Spiritual Life According to Saint Isidore of Seville.* Washington: Catholic University of America Press, 1940.

Nau, F., ed., *Martyrologies et Ménologes Orientaux, vol 10.* Paris: Firmin-Didot, 1915.

Nugent, M. Rosamund, *Portrait of the Consecrated Woman in Greek Christian Literature of the First Four Centuries.* Washington: Catholic University of America Press, 1941.

O'Leary, E. DeLacy, *The Saints of Egypt.* London: Macmillan, 1937.

Otis, Leah Lydia, *Prostitution in Medieval Society.* Chicago: University Press, 1985.

Pagels, Elaine. The Gnostic Gospels. New York: Vintage Books, 1981.

Pagels, Elaine, *Adam, Eve, and the Serpent.* New York: Random House, 1988.

Palladius, *The Lausiac History,* transl. Robert T. Meyer. London: Longmans, Green & Co., 1965.

Patrologiae Cursus Completus, Series Latina, ed. Migne. Belgium: Brepois, 1844–55 (cited as *PL*).

Payer, P. J., "Early Medieval Regulations Concerning Marital Sex Relations," *Journal of Medieval History* 6 (1980), pp. 353–76.

Payer, P. J., *Sex and the Penitentials.* Toronto: University Press, 1984.

Petroff, Elizabeth, "Medieval Women Visionaries: Seven Stages to Power," *Frontiers* 3 (1978), pp. 34–45.

Pharr, Clyde, transl., *The Theodosian Code.* Princeton, NJ: University Press, 1952.

Pomeroy, Sarah B., *Goddesses, Whores, Wives and Slaves: Women in Classical Antiquity.* New York: Schocken Books, 1975.

Pseudo-Clement, "Two Epistles Concerning Virginity," in *The Ante-Nicene Fathers,* vol. III, ed. A. Roberts and J. Donaldson. Grand Rapids, MI: W. B. Eardmans Publishing Co., 1951.

Quasten, Johannes, *Patrology,* vol. l. Brussels: Spectrum Publishers, 1950.

Radar, Rosemary, *Breaking Boundaries: Male/Female Friendship in Early Christian Communities.* New York: Paulist Press, 1983.

Radcliff-Umstead, *Human Sexuality in the Middle Ages and Renaissance.* Pittsburgh, PA: University of Pittsburgh Publications on the Middle Ages and the Renaissance, 1978.

Rampolla del Tindaro, M., *Santa Melania Guiniore Senatrice Romana.* Rome: Tipografia Vaticana, 1905.

Rampolla del Tindaro, M., *Life of St Melania,* transl. E. Leaky. London: Burns & Oates Ltd, 1908.

Rouselle, Aline, *Porneia: De la maîtrise du corps à la privation sensorielle IIᵉ-IVᵉ siècles de l'ère chrétienne.* Paris: Presses Universitaires de France, 1983.

Rouselle, Aline, *Porneia: On Desire and the Body in Antiquity.* Oxford: Basil Blackwell, 1988.

Rousseau, Philip, *Ascetics, Authority and the Church in the Age of Jerome and Cassian.* Oxford: University Press, 1978.

Ruether, Rosemary R., *Religion and Sexism; Images of Women in the Jewish and Christian Traditions.* New York: Simon & Schuster, 1974.

Ruether, R. and McLaughlin, E., eds, *Women of Spirit: Female Leadership in the Jewish and Christian Traditions*. New York: Simon & Schuster, 1979.

Russell, Jeffrey Burton, *A History of Medieval Christianity – Prophecy and Order*. New York: Thomas Y. Crowell, 1971.

Salisbury, Joyce E., "Fruitful in Singleness," *Journal of Medieval History* 8 (1982), pp. 97–106.

Salisbury, Joyce E., *Iberian Popular Religion, 600 BC to 700 AD: Celts, Romans and Visigoths*. New York: Edwin Mellen Press, 1985.

Schiavone de Cruz-Saenz, Michele, *The Life of Saint Mary of Egypt*. Barcelona: Puvill, 1979.

Shaw, Brent D., "The Family in Late Antiquity: The Experience of Augustine," *Past and Present* 115 (May 1987), pp. 3–51.

Simons, G. L., *A Place for Pleasure: the History of the Brothel*. London: Harwood-Smart Publishing, 1975.

Smith Lewis, Agnes, "The Life of Euphrosyne of Alexandria," *Vox Benedictina* (July 1984), pp. 140–56.

Smith Lewis, Agnes, *Select Narratives of Holy Women: Syriac Text, Studia Sinaitica X*. London: C. J. Clay & Sons, 1900.

Smith, William, *A Dictionary of Christian Biography*. New York: AMS Press, 1967.

Springer, M. Theresa, *Nature-Imagery in the Works of Saint Ambrose*. Washington: Catholic University of America Press, 1931.

Stuard, Susan Mosher, ed., *Women in Medieval Society*. Philadelphia, PA: University of Pennsylvania Press, 1976.

Tavard, George H., *Woman in Christian Tradition*. Notre Dame: University Press, 1973.

Tertullian, *Disciplinary, Moral and Ascetical Works*, ed. Roy J. Deferrari. New York: Fathers of the Church, Inc., 1959.

Tertullian, *The Ante-Nicene Fathers, v. IV*, ed. A. Roberts and J. Donaldson. Grand Rapids, MI: W. B. Eardmans Publishing Co., 1951.

The Symposum: A Treatise on Chastity, transl. Herbert Musurillo. Westminster, MD: Newmann Press, 1958.

Torres Rodriguez, Casimiro, "Peragrinaciones de Galicia a Tierra Santa en el s. V," *Compostellanum* (April–June 1956), pp. 401–48.

Usener, Hermann, *Legenden der Heiligen Pelagia*. Bonn: A. Marcus, 1879.

Valerius of Bierzo, "S. Valerii Abbatis opuscula", *PL* 87: 431–7.

Veyne, Paul, "Homosexuality in Ancient Rome," in *Western Sexuality: Practice and Precept in Past and Present Times*, ed. P. Ariès and A. Béjin. Oxford: Basil Blackwell, 1985.

Vita Sancti Ambrosii, transl. Sister Mary Simplicia Kaniecka. Washington: Catholic University of America Press, 1928.

Vita Sanctae Pelagiae, *PL* 73: 663–72.

Vita Sanctae Euphrosynae, Virginis, *PL* 73: 643–52.

Vizmanos, P. Francisco de B., *Las Virgenes cristianas de la iglesia primitiva*. Madrid: Biblioteca de autores cristianos, 1949.

Waddell, Helen J., *The Desert Fathers*. New York: Sheed & Ward, 1942.

Wemple, Suzanne, *Women in Frankish Society: Marriage and the Cloister 500 to*

900. Philadelphia, PA: University of Pennsylvania Press, 1985.
Wilkinson, John, transl., *Egeria's Travels*. London: SPCK, 1971.

Index